THE ASA
BETTER S

THE ASA
GUIDE TO BETTER
SWIMMING

EDITED BY RICK CROSS

Photographs by Michael King

Pan Books London, Sydney and Auckland

Contents

ADRIAN MOORHOUSE

Foreword

Adrian Moorhouse
1985 European 100-metre Breaststroke
Gold Medallist
1986 Commonwealth 200-metre
Breaststroke Gold Medallist
1986 Commonwealth 100-metre
Breaststroke Silver Medallist
Feb 1987 World Record (Short Course)
100-metre Breaststroke
He is the first person to have broken the
60-second mark for 100 metres
breaststroke; he did it in 59.75 seconds

I have always been happy in water, and that is how everybody should be. Swimming is important because it can save lives, those of other people as well as your own; but above all swimming is *fun*. From my first feel of water, to a stage nowadays where I seem to spend more time in than out of it, I have enjoyed every aspect.

I started at the age of four when my parents took me down to the local pool so that I could learn to swim. Soon it became apparent that it was the best way to keep me quiet for an afternoon! At first I learnt how to stay afloat, then progressed to the basic strokes. I joined the swimming club based at the pool, training just once a week, and by the age of nine I had taken part in my first race, winning the local backstroke championship. So from an early age I was involved in the competitive swimming scene. This is the area I have devoted myself to since then – 'devotion' being the operative word, as the training demands are very high. But the rewards are there, and I have had more than my fair share.

I spent much of my time between the ages of nine and fourteen being one of the 'also-rans', probably because I was attempting almost every other sport –

7

rugby, cricket and water polo – as well as training for swimming. At the age of fourteen, however, I moved to the City of Leeds Swimming Club, and because of the heavy training schedule I concentrated solely on swimming. My reward came within six months. I won the national title for my age group in the 200 metres breaststroke, only the third race that I had ever swum at that distance.

Improvement came in leaps and bounds. I made the England Junior Team in the same year as my debut on the British Senior Team at the age of fifteen. I was literally thrown in at the deep end!

The rewards for the hard training are not only the thrill of winning the race and being presented with a medal, but everything else that goes with this. Travel and friendship are two of the important things – from the friends I train with at Leeds, to the friends from other countries whom I race against; from travelling to a local pool in Yorkshire to a marathon journey to Australia to compete in the Commonwealth Games in 1982. It is important to realize that competitive swimming is not a lonely sport. Probably you think of incredibly punishing training, in a cold pool early in the morning . . . well, you are not on your own; there are many other people doing the same thing in your club and all over the world. So the travel opportunities are a reward. My first competitions with the England Youth Squad at the age of fifteen were in Denmark and the South of France. Since then I have been all over the world with my sport. I have been invited to Russia, Hong Kong and the USA to train with various squads, and I have taken part competitively in the Commonwealth Games, European Championships, the Olympic Games and World Championships. You need all the inoculations, but that is a minor price to pay!

There have been many highlights in my career – and swimming has given me memorable moments, mostly good ones. Of course, being involved in high-level competitions for seven years, there have also been disappointments. In experiencing both, I have gained greater motivation. But there is only one experience which sums up what it is all about for me – having the gold medal around my neck and watching the British flag raised to the sound of the National Anthem.

Swimming, for me, is all this. Once you have passed the initial stage of being happy in the water, then you can achieve at any level. This book sets out the possibilities, but only *you* have the potential.

JOHN VERRIER

Introduction

History and organization of the ASA

(*Above*) *Johnny Weissmuller, Paris Olympics, 1924. He won five gold medals, set twenty-four world records, and retired to become a film star*

(*Opposite*) *Berlin Olympics, 1936; Los Angeles Olympics, 1984. Swimming today has been revolutionized by the application of technology — costume difference alone shows this*

John Verrier is Education Officer of the ASA

Rules governing the sport of swimming, including the code for 'games for football in water', were first agreed in 1869; and the Amateur Swimming Association was formed in 1886. It grew quickly and today approximately 1,700 clubs are affiliated, with 300,000 swimmers. Nine million people swim regularly.

In 1869 there was one national championship, and that was the mile. Nine years later the 100 yards and the 500 yards events were added. The first women's championship, the 100 yards, was not swum until 1901. Diving had its own separate association until 1935, when the ASA Diving Committee was formed and took over the work of the Amateur Diving Association. Synchronized swimming competitions were held in 1969, although there had been a specialized club as early as 1961. So there are four competitive branches of the ASA: swimming, diving, synchro – as it is usually called – and water polo, a popular game which grew from football in water.

Today the organization is like a pyramid, the base being formed by the clubs.

11

Above them are the County Associations which are formed into five self-governing districts – South, West, Midland, North, and North East. The ASA's governing body is at the top. European swimming is controlled by LEN (European Swimming Federation), which in turn is a member of the world governing body FINA (Fédération Internationale de Natation Amateur). At the Olympic Games all swimming events are held under FINA laws. The ASA is thus part of a world-wide organization.

Many people do not realize that the ASA is the governing body for swimming in England only. Wales and Scotland have their own Amateur Swimming Associations. The three countries form the Great Britain Federation and compete together in the Olympics, but separately for the Commonwealth Games. Ulster, although part of the United Kingdom, combines with Eire and always swims as Ireland in international events.

The ASA's responsibilities

The ASA governs competitive swimming in England. Through its laws it ensures uniform control of competitions – the objective being, of course, equality and fairness for all competitors. Today, the programme for women is almost the same as that for men, and both embrace the four strokes: backstroke, breaststroke, butterfly and front crawl. I sometimes think that the term 'swimming' does not completely describe the athletic demands and training needed for all four. Diving is close to trampolining and gymnastics, synchronized swimming to dance and gymnastics, while water polo has much in common with basketball. Of course, swimming must be learnt before any of the other three disciplines can be attempted.

The ASA provides competitive and non-competitive swimming activities for all age ranges. There is a full range of competitions for boys and girls aged 12–18 years in swimming and diving, and 12–16 years in synchronized swimming. Water polo has a boys' championship and a county junior championship, while there is a rapid growth in women's water polo as well as an expanding women's championship. The youth of the nation is well catered for.

However, the competitive side of swimming – often referred to as the 'shop window' of the ASA – is by no means the extent of its activities and the vast amount of work done for the general public is sometimes overlooked. There is a tremendous commitment to education. First, the ASA's objective is to have every person a swimmer, and the organization is proud of the fact that much effort has gone into promoting swimming for those with

special needs. Second, it provides instructional classes for teachers and coaches in all four disciplines, as well as meeting special-need requirements. The latest development has been in the provision of water activities for parents and very young children.

The education programmes provide awards which determine abilities and standards. In 1985, over 114,000 Bronze Swimming Challenge Awards were taken by children; and this is but one of the many awards under the control of the ASA. In the same year, 5,656 adults took the Preliminary Teaching Award, which is the first rung on the ASA's ladder of qualifications for becoming a teacher of swimming.

Thus the ASA supervises the activities in the water of babies as young as three months, and veterans turned seventy-five years of age, as well as those participating in world-class competition. It is a healthy, growing organization.

Another development is masters' swimming. A group of events including relays is open to everyone, and they are arranged in five-year steps between the ages of twenty-five and seventy-four years. Group 'L' is the last one, which is for veterans of seventy-five and over. Masters' swimming has grown so rapidly that there are now European and World Championships; they are swum competitively, but they also stimulate a tremendous sociability and rapport, plus not a little nostalgia!

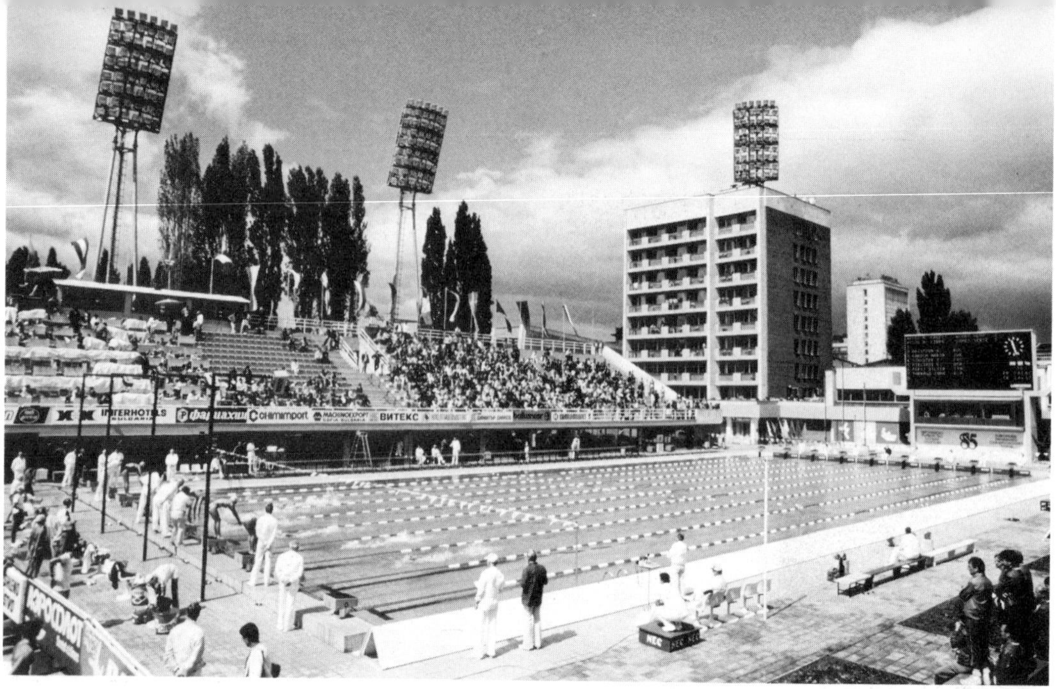
INTERHOTELS
Chimimport
ВИТЕКС

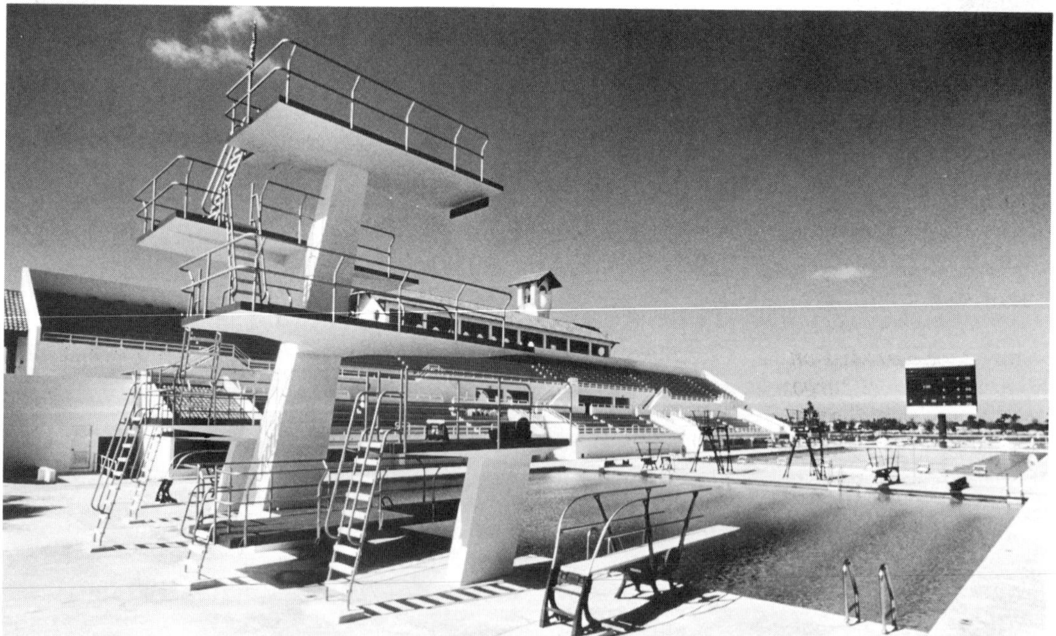

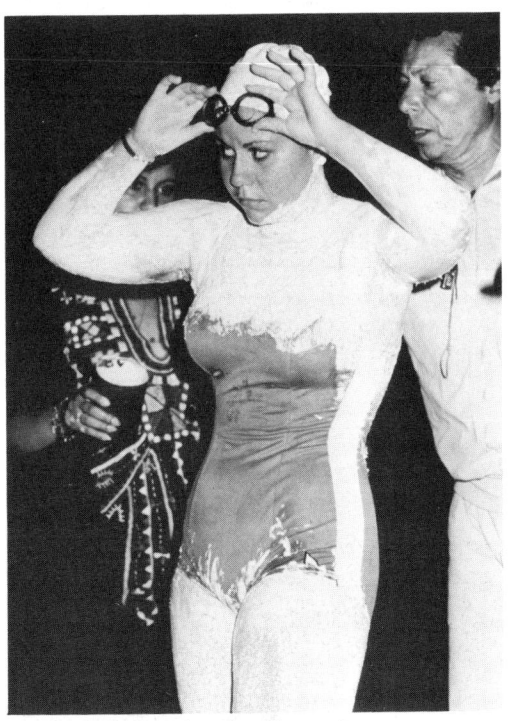

(Above) Swimming the Channel

(Opposite above) Sofia, 1985 European Championships

(Opposite below) Mission Bay, Florida: 'Currently the best purpose-built swimming/ diving complex in the world'

Leisure and safety

The leisure activities of the nation are expanding. Medical opinion favours swimming for sound reasons. It is cheap and requires only a towel and a costume, with perhaps other readily available accessories such as goggles. It can be enjoyed as a family outing. The ability to swim is necessary to many areas of employment, such as the police force, the armed forces or working for an airline. And it saves lives. With the right training, swimming makes it possible for you to help others in trouble, should the need arise. It also enables you to take part in a very wide range of sports such as water-skiing, sailing, canoeing, sub-aqua, wind-surfing and more. You can do all this in greater safety, provided, of course, that you take the appropriate sensible precautions. Do not forget the dangers – but enjoy your swimming.

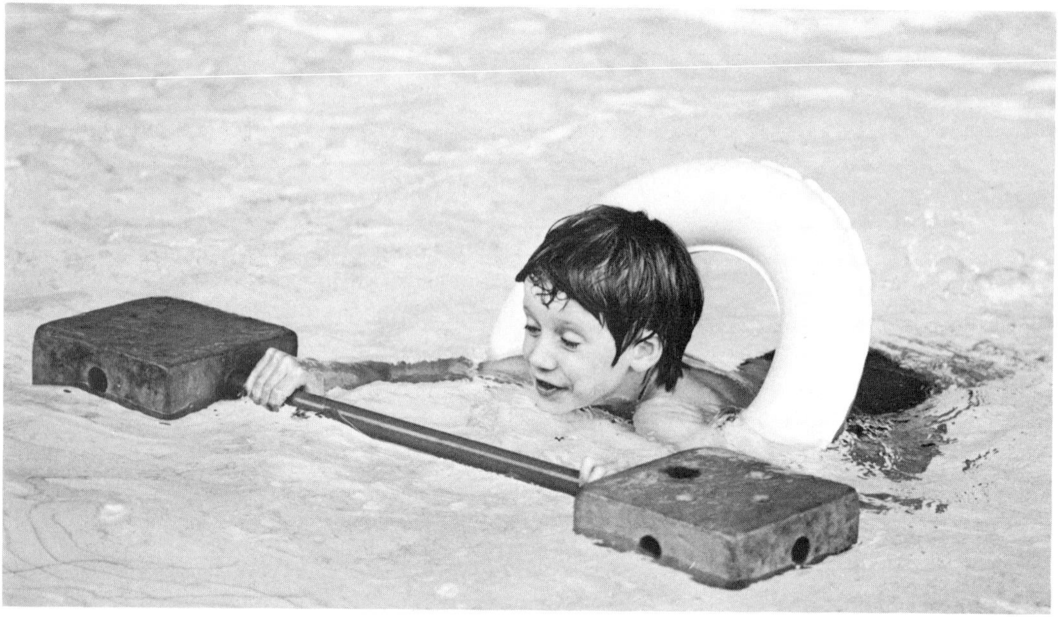

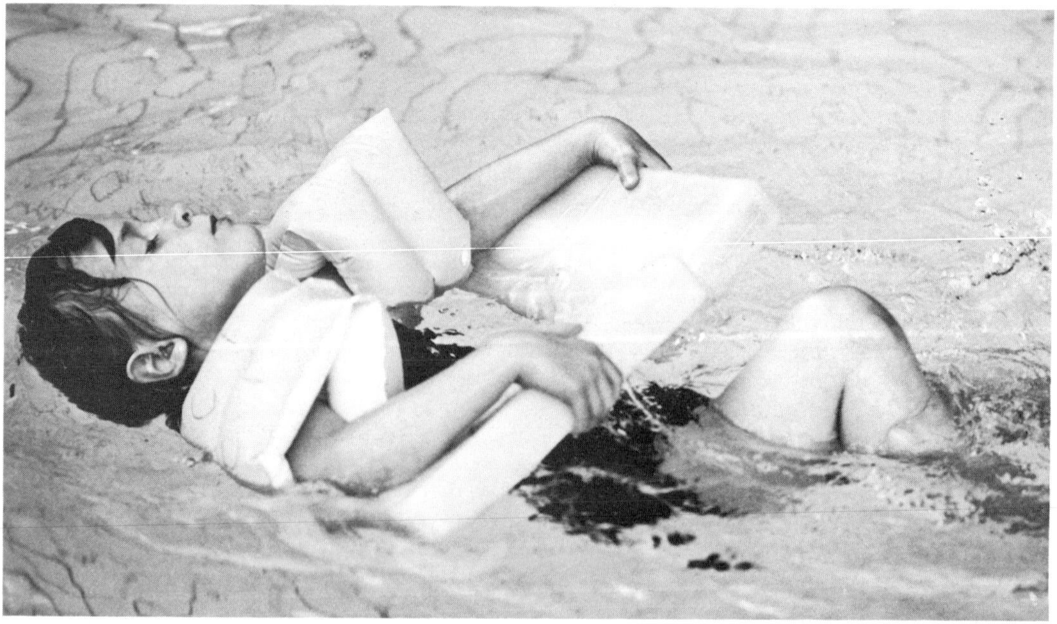

JOAN HARRISON

Part One: Learning to swim – the fundamentals

Early Games, Learning in the Water and Safety

MAKING IT FUN

I have been involved in many sports but still find swimming one of the most satisfying, for it offers relaxation, fun, hard physical work and challenge. Of course the correct introduction to the water is important because it establishes the right habits for future development. Don't be in a hurry to learn the strokes; just take time to become orientated to this new and strange environment. Many parents, I find, expect their children to 'swim' after the first few lessons, and although this is possible, in rushing things they can develop faults which are hard to eradicate. By following a water-orientation programme with progressive watermanship activities, I can give any non-swimmer balance and confidence in the water and a sound foundation for learning the strokes.

Joan Harrison is the Chairperson of the ASA Education Committee; Director of the Sunderland Polytechnic/ASA Swim Centre and an ASA Staff Tutor

A variety of swimming aids

Entering down the steps – backwards for safety

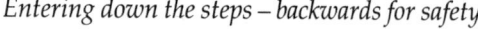

In each session at the pool I give a variety of activities which develop entry skills, floating and gliding, breath control and submerging, travelling, plus creative movement and games.

This section will give progressive practices under each of these, and it is useful to follow the check-list at the end to record your progress through each activity, initially with buoyancy aids and subsequently without. There is a wide range of swimming aids available and their selection should take into consideration cost, versatility, ease of fitting and durability. For the early learning stages, swimming aids should enable the body to assume a horizontal position on the front or back and allow freedom of limb movement. I find armbands meet these criteria and are suitable for all ages. A polystyrene float is a particularly useful aid at all stages for part

stroke practices. Whatever swimming aids are selected, try them on before going to the pool, or use those recommended by the teacher; but in every session there should be time spent without aids so as to avoid over-reliance on them. Once suitable aids are fitted, it is easy to move freely in the water and join in activities and games.

I have known many people who have taught themselves to swim, and this book will help you to do that. It is, however, better and more fun to join a group for instruction or to seek help from a friend who is a competent swimmer. **Don't ever go in the water alone.** I like non-swimmers to attend regularly, if possible every day, even if it is for just a short time. This regular attendance results in learning more quickly, and furthermore some exercise every day is good for you. Swimming is an excellent form of exercise.

18

The First Visit

For the first visit I let the swimmer enter the water down the steps on the pool side, and encourage them to walk away and then bob up and down, immersing the body over the shoulders and adjusting to the water temperature. After the first visit I encourage different ways of entering the water. Try sitting with your legs in the water and twisting and stretching across your body to put both hands firmly on the poolside. Then take the weight of your body on your arms as you slide into the water facing the edge.

Entering from sitting. Place your hands across your body, turn round and lower yourself into the water

It is useful, and also looks better, to be able to enter from a standing position on the poolside. Begin by just stepping into the water, which should be at least shoulder depth. This soon develops into a jump, keeping the head up and letting the

19

knees give when the feet touch the bottom of the pool. If you have a partner to hold one or both hands when first attempting the standing entry, it overcomes any initial fear. Practise the different entries, but do not attempt to go in head-first until you have learnt to swim in the deep water. After each entry, try to climb out rather than going to the steps: place both hands on the poolside, shoulder-width apart: push from the pool bottom to take the weight of your body up and on to the pool side; then lie on the side on your upper body, swing your knee on to the side and wriggle round. The secret is in timing the push with your arms and the push with your legs followed by a bend at the hips.

One of the most pleasant feelings is just to lie supported by the water. This is floating, and it is also an important safety skill. I encourage floating in the prone (on the front) and supine (on the back) positions and then regaining the standing

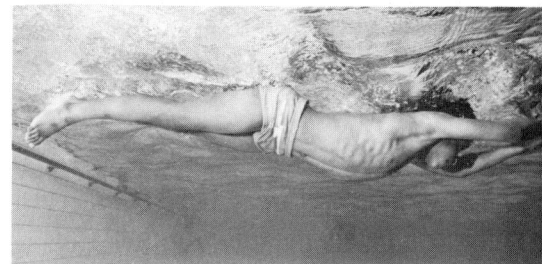

Pushing and gliding in a long thin streamlined shape

Making shapes

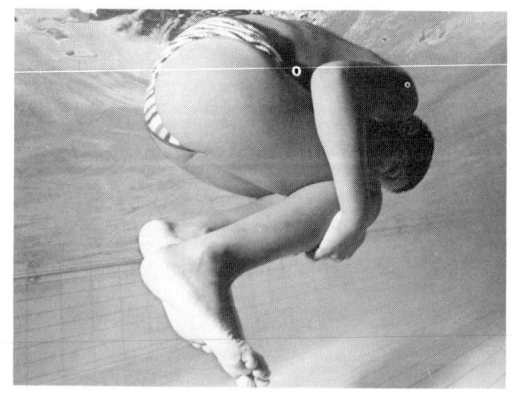

A mushroom float

position in the first pool session: it is a real confidence-boost. Wearing buoyancy aids and with a polystyrene float in each hand, begin by lifting the feet off the bottom into a tucked position, as though sitting in a chair, then returning the feet to the pool bottom. Once balance is achieved in this sitting position I encourage the swimmers to see where they can take their legs to achieve a variety of sitting and lying positions – star shape, thin shape, legs to the side, behind and in front, regaining the standing position by lifting the head, pushing down on the floats and tucking the legs back underneath to the sitting position. It helps to make these movements forceful but not rushed. I find that restful music to accompany these floating activities helps the swimmer to relax and take it easy.

The next stage is to achieve floating without the polystyrene floats, gradually putting the head into the water when in the prone position. To stand up, it is now

Regaining standing position

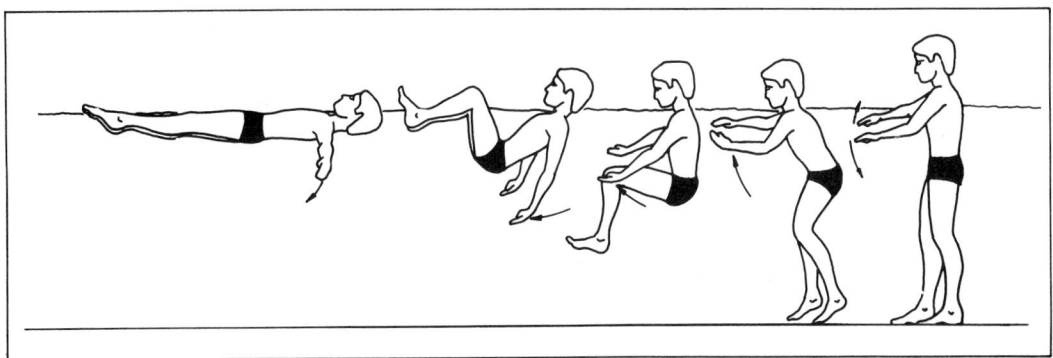

necessary to add an arm movement, pressing down with the hands from the prone position, and scooping the arms down to the sides and up to the surface from the supine position. Floating is an important safety skill for all swimmers. Whether the float is vertical or horizontal, it is a good resting position. Having learnt to float and stand up, it is now an easy progression to glide through the water. The body travels more easily if it assumes a long, thin, streamlined shape; it is easy to find this out. Push from the side of the pool into a stretched glide position, then a wide position, then a tucked position. A partner in front can help you to stand up if needed, but can also note the length of each glide.

Early skills

Once the streamlined position is achieved in the glides, the basic balance for all swimming strokes is learnt. I tell my swimmers always to feel long and thin, with the arms pressed forward close to the ears and the feet stretched up to the water surface. Complete the progression in this section by combining pushing and gliding, stopping in a floating shape and standing up. It is important to be aware of the shape your whole body is making on each movement and to feel the water passing the body on the strong streamlined glide.

Sculling is another important safety skill which can be used to balance the body, maintain a static position or give propulsion. Begin by floating on your back (supine) with the arms stretched to the sides and the hands close to or under the hips. By constantly tipping the hands so that

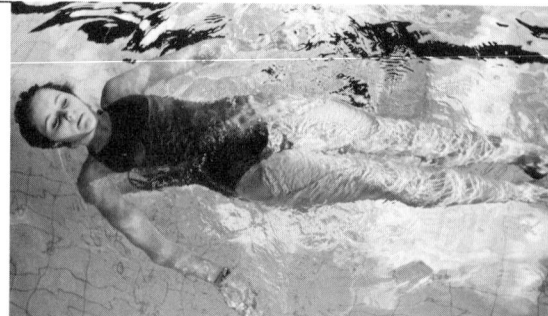

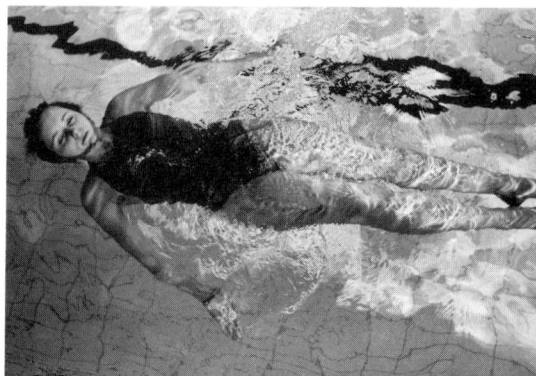

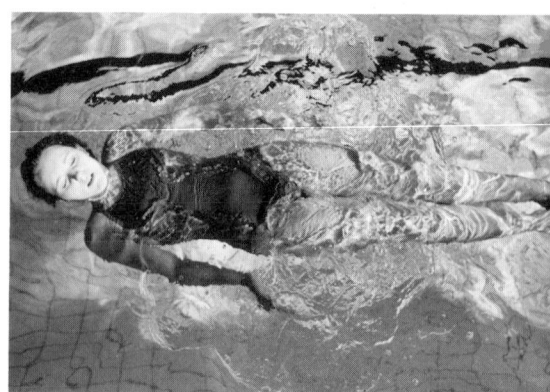

Sculling: constantly tip the hands so that they move in and out from the wrist and give a firm downward pressure

they move in and out from the wrist, they give a firm downward pressure. The faster and more constant the movement, the more efficient it is. The body should remain on the spot but high in the water. It is possible to try slowly lifting one knee, keeping the foot in the water; you will find you have to scull harder to maintain this position.

This same sculling action is the basis of another safety skill – treading water. Wearing buoyancy aids, let the body hang in a vertical position. Lifting the feet from the pool bottom, with the palms of the hands facing down, scull the hands in front of you. Again the pressure is downward to keep the body up with the head out of the water for easy breathing. Add a leg action. Kicking, circling or moving as though walking upstairs will help to keep you up.

Breathing

Many swimmers have said to me, 'Yes, I can swim, but I find it difficult to breathe and I am afraid to put my head in the water.' I try to achieve aquatic breathing and submerging in this early watermanship programme. The first stage can be done at home in the bath (no soap!) just blowing bubbles in the water by blowing out hard with the mouth under the surface, then putting the face on the surface, opening the eyes and blowing bubbles. On first entering the pool, begin by taking the water to your face as if washing it, or pouring water over your head, and doing the same blowing-out activities as tried at home, always concentrating on blowing

out through both the nose and the mouth.

Once confidence is gained to wet the face, I go on to a variety of submerging activities. I advise opening the eyes once under the water, as they tend to close automatically when passing under the sur-

Swimming underwater needs to be learnt step by step

23

face. Bobbing up and down, and jumping up and down while trying to sit on the bottom of the pool are all good fun. Touch the bottom of the pool with different parts of your body, then try to recover objects from under water, or go through a hoop or the legs of a partner. Once the swimmer is able to glide by pushing along the water surface, I encourage pushing and gliding under water, dropping the head down and lifting the hips high to help submersion, and at the end of the glide placing the feet on the floor of the pool to give a strong push back up to the surface. Doing these activities with a partner encourages opening the eyes under water – 'try to look at your partner', eventually becoming 'travel under water with a partner'.

Travelling

The aim of swimming is to travel efficiently in water in a variety of ways. Just begin by experimenting to find different ways of travelling in all directions. We have already established that the body should be high in the water and streamlined, and that the arms and legs give the main propulsion by pulling and pushing against the resistance of the water. On first entering the water begin to walk with long steps forwards, then backwards and sideways. The resistance of the water will be felt against the legs and body: keep the shoulders under and help the motion and balance of the body by pushing and pulling with the arms. Try moving in the water, jogging and jumping on the spot; it is good for stamina and not as hard on the legs as jogging and jumping when on

land. As you walk or run, gradually lift the legs higher and lean forward – the legs will begin to rise and kick behind you.

From a prone glide position with the hands holding a float or a ball, use the legs to propel the body. If using a kicking action, think about long legs and flipper-like feet; if using a circular action, push the water with flat feet and keep the circle narrow. Try propelling yourself in the same way but from a supine glide position, with a float or ball held above the chest or hips. The next step is to find out how the arms act as levers to move the body through the water. Keeping your arms under the water, use them to perform an alternate dog or front paddle action or a simultaneous circular action, pulling your body through the water. Add any leg action to help balance the body and you are moving on your front.

I find many swimmers prefer moving from a supine glide position as it is easier to breathe. Use a back paddle action to push the water towards the feet, or a sculling action. By adding one of the leg actions already tried, you will find swimming on the back is easy. Don't forget: lift the head, bend the knees and sweep the arms to regain standing. You can find out more about the 'paddle' strokes in the next section.

The swimmer finds the next stage of moving in the water by experimenting. Put together different arm and leg actions and try to travel with feet leading or head leading, by turning sideways on the spot

(Opposite) Front paddle, often known as doggy paddle. A circular action, down and backwards, pulls you through the water

24

and turning when travelling, and move under water as well as on the surface. By now you ought to be really confident in water. Always remember, push or pull the water in the opposite direction to that in which you are going to travel. Try to increase the distance covered without stopping and gradually reduce the air in the buoyancy aids. Then dispense with them completely. I recommend working with a partner when first going without swimming aids. The partner just walks ahead to help if needed, but this does help the new swimmer to feel confident.

Fun and games in the water

Games

Playing games and having races can make the learning stages more fun and I use the games we have all played on land. Keep buoyancy aids on so that it is easy to move and become thoroughly involved without any fear. Throw and catch a ball alone, with a partner or in circle or a line. Play 'pig-in-the-middle', or two-versus-two, counting how many passes are made before an interception. Throwing and catching relays are good competitive small-team games. Construct a team of, say, only four members, so there is plenty of activity. I ask teams to make up their own games or races using the skills which have been learnt and selected apparatus, like hoops, balls or weighted objects that sink. I also encourage making sequences of skills from their repertoire – such as

pushing and prone gliding, then rotating to a supine position, travelling and stopping in a wide shape. Or, travelling on the front, travelling under water up to the surface and sculling to the side and climbing out. These sequences can be performed to music and with a partner or in a small group. This is the start of synchronized swimming – you can read more about it in Part 3.

If these progressive stages have been followed carefully, swimmers fully understand how to move in water and have the confidence and skill necessary to go on to learn specific stroke patterns, diving (see Part 3), and other more advanced movements in water. Do take these early stages carefully. It makes the learning of strokes so easy.

WATERMANSHIP PERSONAL SKILLS CHECK LIST

STARTING DATE

SKILL	WITH SWIMMING AIDS DATE	WITHOUT SWIMMING AIDS DATE
ENTERING AND LEAVING THE WATER		
1 Down the steps		
2 Sit and swivel		
3 Stand and step in		
4 Jump in		
5 Climb out		
BALANCING, FLOATING, GLIDING		
6 Prone float – curled		
7 – wide		
8 – long and thin		
9 Regain standing from a prone float		
10 Supine float – wide		
11 – long and thin		
12 – any other shape		
13 Regain standing from supine float		
14 Prone push, glide and stand up		
15 Supine push, glide and stand up		

Learning to swim – the fundamentals

SKILL	WITH SWIMMING AIDS DATE	WITHOUT SWIMMING AIDS DATE
16 Sculling keeping the body up		
17 Treading water		
18 Gliding or floating, changing prone to supine		
19 Gliding or floating, changing supine to prone		
BREATHING AND SUBMERGING		
20 Face on the water eyes open		
21 Blowing bubbles in the water		
22 Face submerged, exhale		
23 Touching pool floor		
24 Picking up object from pool floor		
25 Sitting on pool floor, exhale		
26 Going through a submerged hoop		
27 Moving underwater		
TRAVELLING		
28 Walking – different directions		
29 Jogging		
30 Jumping		
31 Prone glide using legs to travel		
32 Prone glide using arms to travel		

SKILL	WITH SWIMMING AIDS DATE	WITHOUT SWIMMING AIDS DATE
33 Prone glide using arms and legs to travel		
34 Supine glide using legs to travel		
35 Supine glide using arms to travel		
36 Supine glide using arms and legs to travel		

GAMES, LINKED MOVEMENTS, FURTHER ACTIVITIES

Record any other activities your are taught or make up yourself

Front and Back Paddle

Although there is no one 'correct' way of teaching youngsters to swim, some methods are more commonly used than others. I frequently find it helpful to get learners moving through the water at an early stage, using the 'doggy' or front paddle. I am sure everyone will at some time have seen a dog fetching a stick out of the water (and have been showered when it eventually emerges and shakes its coat!). Many four-legged animals are competent swimmers over a short distance. The large herds which migrate across Africa frequently have to cross swollen and fast-flowing rivers in order to reach their new grazing grounds.

Nothing succeeds like success and the sooner a beginner starts to move independently through the water, the greater motivation there will be for learning to swim. Front and back paddle enable learners to gain independence in the swimming pool at a comparatively early stage and after a limited amount of practice.

PUSHING, GLIDING AND STANDING UP

I find it is better to let youngsters experience pushing and gliding before they start any limb movements. Some will need the added security of a float, while others will be quite happy to push off from the side of the pool with only armbands to support them. Confidence in pushing and gliding also means that the child will be able to regain a standing position without undue stress. It would be a good idea to look at the illustrations on page 21.

FRONT PADDLE

If the image of a dog paddling through the water is put into the child's mind at the beginning of the lesson, he or she will immediately envisage the actions. I find that the less confident children usually keep one or both feet close to the bottom of the pool on the first few attempts. Bolder

Alan Donlan has been Honorary Secretary to the ASA Education Committee since 1973 children will make the paddling movements with their hands almost automatically. As the name suggests, the hands are moved like the paws of a dog alternately under the surface of the water using a downwards circular motion. During this time the chin is either just above or level with the surface of the water. Children will tend to start with a short arm pull, but after a while will realize that the longer the arm pull, the more relaxed is the stroke. Ideally, at this stage, the legs should alternately kick, like the front crawl stroke. However, some children will introduce their own unique leg action which can gradually be converted. If a child is excessively timid, progress will take considerably longer. It might help initially to have such a child walking parallel to the side of the pool with the water below shoulder depth and at the same time 'pawing' the water with alternate arms. The child can then be encouraged to do the action faster; automatically, the feet will then have shorter contact with the bottom of the pool. Those who make a real effort will find that their feet are lifted from the bottom of the pool by the arm action. With timid children, I find it helps to relate every movement to something with which they are already familiar. For example, once they have lost contact with the bottom of the pool, they should be encouraged to 'cycle' with the legs. Slowly but surely, they will begin to assume a more horizontal position at the surface and eventually gain confidence to move across the pool without the wall being close at hand. Later, they can begin to use a straighter leg kick.

Although I find that most children prefer to learn the front paddle first because they can see where they are going, teachers have to be prepared for the individual who is happier starting on the back. Whether using front or back paddle, most children are happier wearing armbands for extra confidence and support.

BACK PADDLE

The back paddle is traditionally a combination of a sculling type action with a leg kick similar to the back crawl action. You can read about sculling on page 22. Gradually you can introduce the alternating up-and-down leg kick to make up the back paddle. Having mastered the front and back paddle, beginners are now able to move fairly confidently and freely in the water. If they have not already dispensed with the armbands and other swimming aids, they should now be encouraged to swim without them. This is best done in stages by releasing air from armbands, until the swimmers find that they can manage without them. It often helps to ask children if they would like to swim without armbands. After some hesitation at first, they will readily make the attempt because swimming without armbands is a major step forward for an enthusiastic youngster.

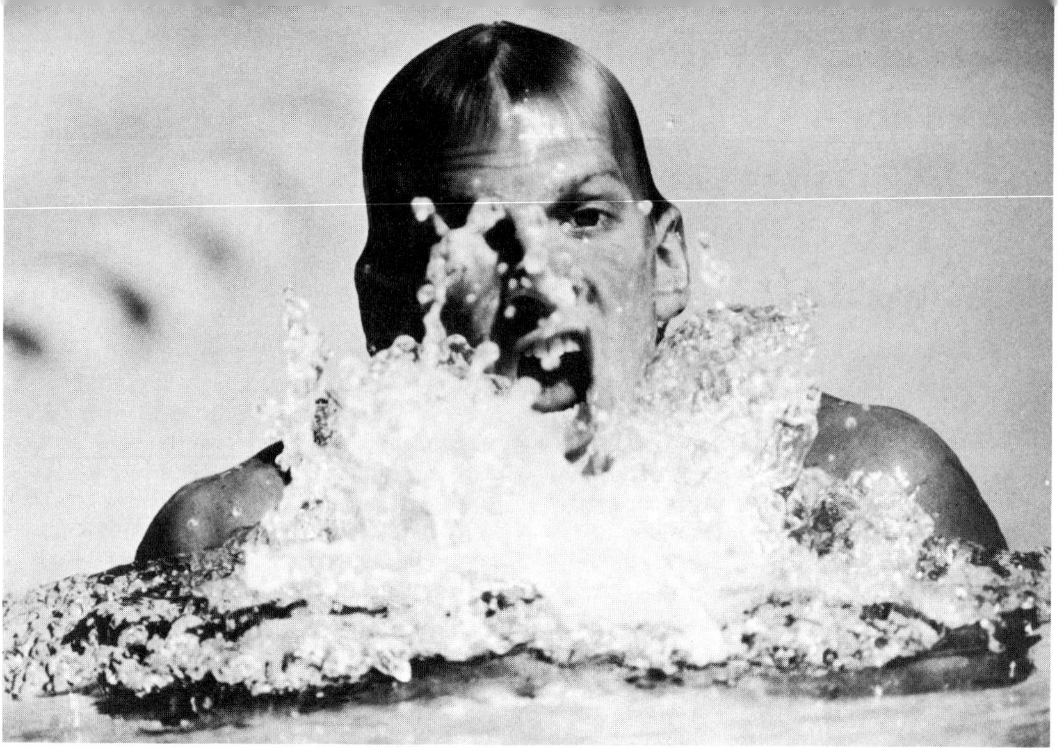

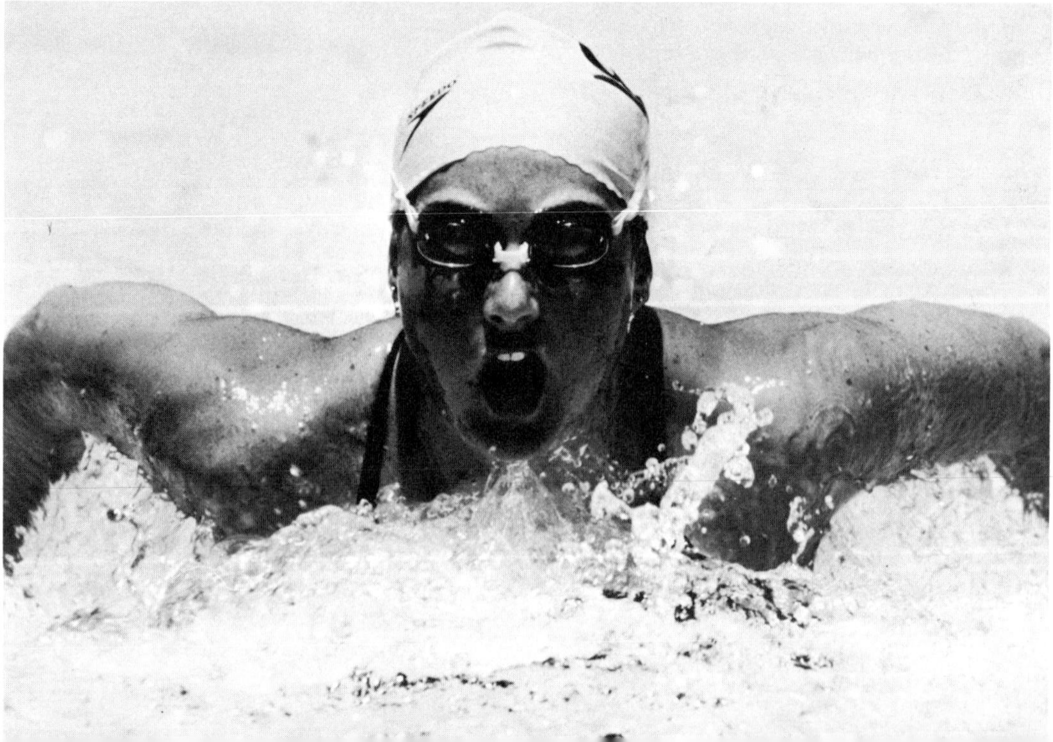
SPEEDO

ANNE CRADOCK

The Multistroke Method

INTRODUCTION

If you are a non-swimmer, and you have learned to regain your feet from a floating position on your front and back (see page 21), or you can push yourself in a flat gliding position through the water from the pool floor or the pool wall (with or without swimming aids), you are ready to learn the basics of the three main strokes: front crawl, back crawl and breaststroke.

Like many teachers, my main aim is to help people to find methods of moving through the water with ease and confidence, and to develop safety skills through enjoyment and fun. I prefer to introduce these three strokes at a basic level, alongside each other, with equal time and emphasis given to each. It soon becomes obvious to both pupil and teacher which stroke is the most natural to that individual; later, the chosen stroke will be given more emphasis. This approach is known as the multistroke method.

THE BASICS OF THE STROKES

You may ask, 'What are the basics of these strokes?' A detailed analysis of each stroke can be found later in the book, but at this early stage the strokes may be practised as follows.

Americans Steve Lundquist and Mary Meagher: both gold medallists at the 1984 Olympics.

An ASA Staff Tutor, Anne Cradock holds teaching certificates in swimming for the disabled and synchronized swimming. She is also a Royal Life Saving Society advanced teacher and a grade 1 examiner

Initially, **front crawl** is known as front paddle or dog paddle. You can read about this on page 30. Remember, your arms stay in the water all the time in front paddle, alternately sliding forward to a position ahead of your body and pulling down and back towards the centre of your body. It is a natural alternating movement like walking. You can breathe freely and see where you are going, as your face is clear of the water.

Back crawl at this stage is known as back paddle. The back of your head rests in the water with your eyes looking upwards. Your legs (as in front paddle) are stretched straight out along the surface and kick alternately up and down. Your arms stay in the water alongside your body at present, performing a sculling action. Some people prefer to start swimming on their backs because their face is well clear of the water, although it is difficult to see where you are going.

Breast stroke can be a relaxing, slower stroke and is chosen by many adult learners for this reason, although the coordination is more difficult and the ankle position less natural than the other strokes. The arm action is under the water all the time and can be practised by walking with your shoulders under the water and your chin on the water, keeping your head still. Stretch your arms ahead of your body (under the water) and pull both arms around and back, drawing a circular pathway in front of you. Then slide your arms forward to the stretched position again. As your arms are sliding forward, both your heels are pulled up towards your seat with your toes turned outwards. You then kick around and backwards with your heels, drawing a circular pathway under the water surface. As with the other strokes, the leg kicks can be practised on their own by holding a float in front of you. Because of individual physical differences, people may find certain types of movement easier than others.

VARIETY OF MOVEMENT

The multistroke method gives you the opportunity to try all the strokes and choose the movements which you find most natural to practise. These may not necessarily combine together to form a recognized stroke and in the early stages of learning this does not matter. In fact, we refer to these as stroke 'hybrids' and they add variety and fun to a swimming programme as well as providing useful coordination exercises for more able swimmers. For example, the circular breaststroke arm action can be combined with the alternating crawl leg kick, or the alternating front paddle arm action can be combined with the double action breaststroke leg kick. It is not as easy as it sounds – try it! Perhaps you could try the butterfly actions, too. Details appear in a later section of Part 1.

Once you have achieved your first five metres (which is as important to the oldest adult as to the youngest child) you will want your family and friends to accompany you to your local pool to show off what you have learned with your teacher. REMEMBER, NEVER GO ALONE TO THE POOL. In order to prepare my pupils for public swimming sessions where the unexpected often happens, I spend a considerable time teaching them the skills of changing shape, position and direction in the water. These are enjoyable activities which are very important for safety when you are swimming in a public pool and I think this is one of the greatest benefits of the multistroke method.

To practise these skills, start off again with a push and glide on your front and then, before you lose momentum, roll over on to your back by looking up at the ceiling. You may then turn to swim front paddle, and roll on to your back again to continue with back paddle. This might be useful in the middle of the pool where you are doing very nicely until the enthusiastic swimmer doing his eightieth length swamps you with his 'wash' and you need to clear your eyes and have a breather!

In another situation, you are about to swim your first length on your back when someone jumps in just ahead of you, calling for a rapid direction change. This can be achieved quickly by tucking in your knees tightly, lifting your head so that you become upright, then moving rapidly away on your front.

As well as changing from front to back and mixing and matching your arm and leg actions, you should also practise changing direction. Do this by swimming to either side, diagonally and in circular pathways, to enable you to avoid any obstacles. By doing this you will soon become a competent multistroke swimmer. Once your leg kick is strong enough, you will be ready to learn the recognized front and back crawl arm actions with their recovery movements over the water.

The start of the world triathlon championship held annually in Nice, France (the event consists of a two-mile swim, a 100-mile cycling race and a twenty-mile run).

DAVID HICKS

Front Crawl

WHAT IS FRONT CRAWL

Front crawl is the most efficient and therefore the fastest of all swimming strokes. Generally the first stroke taught by teachers, it is a natural action, almost like walking. Beginners usually start with the doggy or front paddle, covered in a previous section. The progression after that is to lie flatter on the water for streamlining and use an over-the-water recovery of the arms for efficiency. Breathing should be to the side and not to the front.

The body should be stretched, just under the surface of the water, on the front and as flat as possible, but allowing for the leg kick. I like to see the head in a natural position, neither lifted nor buried, with the eyes looking forward and downwards. The water surface should be somewhere between the eyebrows and hair line. The head should be steady and central except to breathe. A certain amount of body roll will take place as the strong muscles of the chest assist the arm action from entry to recovery. This body roll is along the length of the body, i.e. the longitudinal axis, and is unavoidable due to pressure being applied by the arms. We must try to avoid sideways or lateral movement, as this will cause resistance to forward motion. In the early stages breath-holding for a short distance is recommended, with the face in the water to establish a good body position.

LEG ACTION

We then look at the leg action and try to develop an efficient leg kick right from the start. The main function of the legs is to

(Opposite) Matt Biondi. 1986 World Championships.

David Hicks is ASA National Development Officer, Crystal Palace National Sports Centre

stabilize the body position and to give a certain amount of propulsion to the strokes as a whole. Sprint swimmers will use and get more power from the legs than the distance swimmers who have to conserve their energies. The legs move in an alternate up and down action fairly close together. The movement starts at the hips then down through the slightly bent knees and ending with a whip-like action at the feet. The feet should be extended from the ankles, i.e. plantar-flexed, which will bring the largest area of the instep and upper surface of the feet in contact with the water pressure in a backward and downward direction. The depth of kick is usually about 30–45 cms (12–18 inches), with most of the pressure developed on the down kick. During the up kick, the soles of the feet and backs of the legs press upwards and backwards against the water, and the legs are straight. The heels should not come out of the water and the flexibility of the ankles will determine the amount of propulsion gained by the legs. So, the legs stabilize the body whilst also providing some propulsion.

ARM ACTION

The arm action is the main propulsive force in front-crawl swimming and is an alternating action with a continuous movement. One arm pulls, while the other one recovers. The hand enters the water thumb or fingers first. I prefer thumbs first, with the hand entering at an angle of 45° between the head and shoulder lines, but not crossing the centre of the body line. The arm is not completely straight with a downward slant from elbow to finger tips. After entry the hand sinks to a catch position, i.e. it takes hold of the water, about 15–21 cm (6–8 in) under the surface and begins exerting downward and backward pressure along the side of, or just under, the body and keeping close to the centre line. The elbow is kept high during this phase, with the wrist flexed and held firm with a maximum bend of 90° at this stage. The palm of hand must face the direction of pull. A bent elbow is more effective than a straight one, as you are closer to the centre line of the body with stronger muscles being used. During the last push phase the hand passes under the body, still facing the direction of the feet until the thumb reaches the thigh. On recovery the elbow leaves the water first and leads the recovery with speed, but in a relaxed state and with the least amount of interference with the stroke. The minimum amount of energy should be used in this non-productive action.

BREATHING

Children seem to adapt to a breathing technique more easily than adults in the learning stage of front crawl. Countless numbers of adults have experienced that problem over the years. Breathing should blend into the stroke with the minimum amount of interference as, again, this contributes nothing to propulsion – except to supply oxygen, of course! The breath should be held during the propulsive phase of the arm action, and taken at the end of the push when one arm is in the 'catch' position and the other just leaving the water. A preference for early or late breathing will depend on the experience of the swimmer. Early breathing occurs in the stroke, i.e. before or as the hand finishes the push back. Later breathing comes as the hand and arm are in the recovery position almost under the armpit. Most competitors use this type of breathing pattern combined with explosive breathing, i.e. blow – suck action when the head is turned into the 'trough' created by the bow wave. The head should not be turned more than is necessary and certainly not lifted at all. As the arm con-tinues the recovery, the head returns to a central position. Most beginners use a trickle breathing method, i.e. breath exhaled through nose and mouth while the face is submerged. Breath is then taken with a gulping action as the mouth surfaces from the water. Bilateral breathing means alternate breathing to both sides, normally every third arm pull. This is useful for correcting faults in the stroke and is essential for competitive swimmers to be able to see the opposition on both sides without breaking the rhythm of the stroke. Breath-holding, or hypoxic training, is used for beginners in establishing an even stroke early in training. This is good conditioning practice, but must be used with caution by experienced coaches and teachers.

GETTING IT TOGETHER

The timing and coordination of front crawl is very important, with each component – arms, legs and breathing – blending together. The number of leg kicks per arm cycle depends on the type of race, distance or sprint, and on the preference of the swimmer. A six-beat leg kick is mostly preferred by young swimmers; as they become more experienced, they might change to a four- or two-beat leg kick.

We have looked at the mechanics of front crawl; now let us consider the different styles of the same technique.

A lot will depend on the body type: short, fat, long, thin, strong, weak and so on. The person who is fat will usually have a lot of buoyancy and will float high, whereas a thin or muscular person will normally sink easily. So we have to adapt our strokes accordingly. A strong person will roll more because of the powerful action of the arms. We normally talk about 35° body roll, but this can be 60° or more. The person with poor flexibility might well recover the arm in a ballistic swinging movement over the water, entering well over the centre line. I would normally expect this type of action to be accompanied by a wide two-beat leg action and some lateral movement of the body. Pulling with a dropped elbow results in less hand area being presented to the water; thus propulsion is reduced considerably. Once the hand has entered the water and 'taken hold' in the catch position, then the action speeds up, ending with a flourish.

This will assist fast recovery, too.

Flexibility in all our joints will help by allowing us a full range of movement throughout the stroke. Another problem experienced by beginners is trying to keep the eyes open during swimming. It is essential to do this for safety reasons, but it should be learned in the early stages of confidence practices. Goggles might assist if there is a medical disorder, or for the competitive swimmer who is training many hours daily.

We have looked at basic mechanics and technique with regard to different styles of swimming front crawl. Now let us see how we build up the stroke for beginners. The push and glide practices mentioned in an earlier section will help to develop a nice flat body position. This should be done with the head in the water, which helps to overcome fears of having the face under water. You use long legs, pointed toes, with not too much bending at the knees and try to initiate the kick from the hips. It is an alternating movement and you can try it with a float held out in front of you to see how effective the leg kick is. At first there may be very little movement forward, but work at it, and with flexible ankles and determined effort you will be surprised how quickly progress can be made. You will see this 'legs only' practice carried out daily by all good swimmers.

Arm practices are best learned as part of the whole stroke. Once push and glide has been attempted and leg action added, try using the arms in the alternating way described without breathing over short distances. Every swimmer has a favourite side to breathe, so find out which yours is and add a breath to that side during the

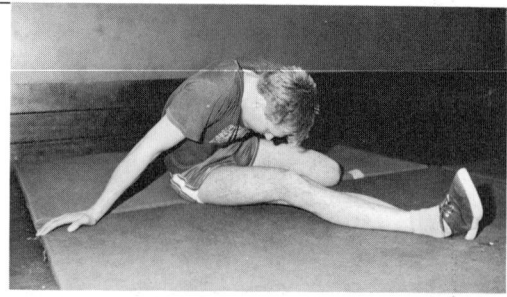

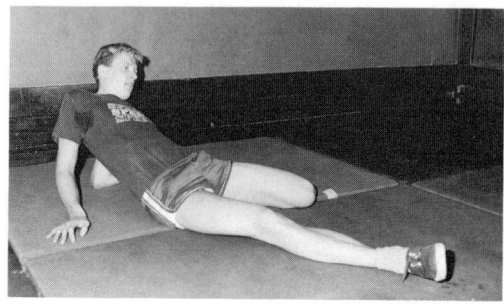

Flexibility in all your joints is vital for a full range of movement

arm cycle. As success shows through, repeat, adding two and more breaths until a pattern develops. The more you practise the better you become, and the more relaxed you are the further you will swim. The further you swim the fitter you become, so you can swim even further. It is an endless, and very enjoyable, cycle. Most of the work done in swim training by competitive swimmers is done on front crawl. As you become proficient in this stroke and want to improve, my advice is to join a swimming club where proper instruction can be given under supervised conditions of safety. Many skills and drills of technique will be practised, may be many times a week. Practice makes perfect, but only the right practice!

FRONT CRAWL

1. After entering the water, the left hand reaches forward to the catch point.

3. Pulling down and back from catch point, the hand passes immediately below the shoulder and moves into the push phase, which takes it back towards the hip. The hand acts like a paddle pushing backwards.

2. The left elbow starts to bend into the most efficient angle for the pull phase of the stroke. The hand forms a firm paddle shape.

4. Almost at the hip, the hand continues to adapt its pitch to maintain the pushing action.

LEGS

Throughout front crawl, the leg action is an alternating up and down kick with minimal knee bending and feet stretched. The feet pass close to each other in the stretched and in-toed position.

BREATHING

The breathing action is demonstrated clearly in pictures 4, 5 and 6. The head is turned sideways so that the mouth is clear of the water for an exchange of air. It then returns to the more streamlined face-down position.

5. *Just prior to exit point, the hand has rotated so that the palm is turned inwards and the little finger leads the hand out of the water. The bent elbow leads the arm as it lifts. This begins the recovery phase.*

6. *The sequence starts again for the right arm. The left arm is in recovery and is over the water's surface.*

7. *This is a front view of the actions in picture 2. Note the firm paddle shape of the hand, and the path it is taking along the body's centre line. The elbow's angle facilitates the strong pull/push action. The left arm here is propulsive, whilst the right arm has completed the recovery phase and is just entering the water.*

FRONT CRAWL TUMBLE-TURN SEQUENCE

1. As the swimmer approaches the wall, the right hand (now at the end of the push phase) remains alongside the hip, whilst the left arm goes through its push phase until it is alongside the left hip. Many swimmers make a short dolphin-type kick to help with the somersaulting rotation.

2. The head drives downwards and the hips move in over the head as the somersault action starts. The hands press downwards to aid the body's rotation.

7. Powerful drive off the wall. The body is in full extension. The longitudinal roll develops as the swimmer moves out and returns to the surface. When he emerges he will be on his front, ready for the first stroke out from the wall.

3. *The somersault continues, hands pressing down further.*

4. *The legs begin to tuck as they are about to move up and over the water's surface.*

6. *The feet make contact. Arms continue to stretch in readiness for the drive off the wall. There is a slight twisting movement to start longitudinal rotation.*

5. *Downward rotation is complete. The feet are about to plant firmly on the wall: the hands prepare to stretch forward.*

45

DAVID SPARKES

Back Crawl

INTRODUCTION

Back crawl is very similar to front crawl. It is one of the many types of backstroke, but with the development of the stroke into an alternating arm and leg action it has become the most effective way of swimming on the back. For this reason back crawl is chosen by our competitive swimmers as the stroke performed in backstroke races, although ASA law does allow any form of backstroke to be swum.

Competitive swimming is not, of course, the only aspect of swimming. Before our stars become stars, they have to learn to swim. I have found that many children and adults prefer back crawl in the early stages, largely because the swimmer can keep his face out of the water and thus experience less difficulty in breathing. One of the main problems experienced when first teaching back crawl is that the swimmer is concerned about his inability to know what is ahead of him unless he turns his head. The head must remain still, for reasons which we will go into later, but it is important that when learning the stroke the pupil is taught to do a **SAFETY** check to see if the way is clear before starting to swim.

BODY POSITION

Let us now look in detail at how to swim back crawl, beginning with the body position. Once again, we are looking for a body position high in the water with the hips just under the surface and shoulders

Betsy Mitchell (USA), world champion in 1986 for 100m and 200m backstroke

An engineer by profession, David Sparkes is also an ASA Staff Tutor and Coach. He serves on a variety of ASA committees

held high. Your head should be held steady with your ears under the surface, as though your head is cushioned on a pillow, while your eyes should be looking upwards and backwards down the pool.

It is important to remember that the key to a good body position is a correct head position. If the head is held too high your legs will drop and be too low, and if you put your head too far back, other problems will arise. Another important point to remember in back crawl is that the head should remain stationary, because any movement will be exaggerated into lateral movement in the body. When viewing back crawl swimmers from head on, you will observe two different types of body position. With some swimmers, the shoulders remain stationary and parallel to the water surface, whereas others roll towards their pulling arm. The degree of roll will vary from swimmer to swimmer, but it is essential that if you wish to perform back crawl in the most efficient manner, body roll should be introduced into the stroke. This will allow you to carry out the correct hand movement during the underwater phase of the arm action, which will then produce the most mechanically effective action. Initially you may find the points mentioned above difficult to achieve; however, as you become more confident and more skilled you must aim for this body position.

ARM ACTION

As with all the other strokes, your powerhouse is in the arms and the key to good swimming is to have a strong, effective arm action. You should aim to develop a continuous arm action without any pauses whatsoever. Your initial entry should be with a straight arm and ideally you should aim to enter the water between the shoulder and the centre body line. Your little finger should enter the water first and the palm of your hand should face outwards.

I have already mentioned that the body position of the swimmer can vary; this is due to the type of underwater phase of the arm action. There are two types of arm action, one which follows a horizontal semi-circular pathway, and one which moves through an 'S' pattern. Let us first look at the underwater phase of the arm action which follows a semi-circular pathway. After entry, the hand should move outwards to gain purchase on the water 15–21 cm (6–8 in) below the surface. The arm should continue to move outwards and backwards with little flexion in the elbow, and follow a semi-circular path within the depth of the body until it reaches the hip. This type of action is used by many swimmers in the early stages and

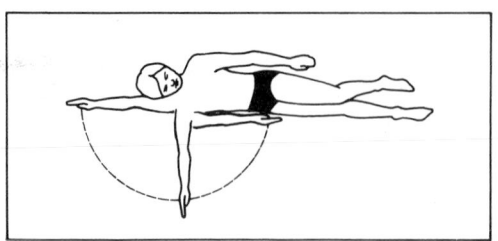

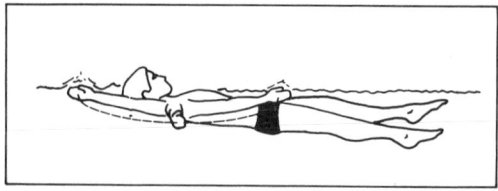

Arm action: a horizontal, circular pathway

by recreational swimmers, but those who wish to perform the stroke more effectively and achieve greater speed will need to adopt the second arm action, which is often referred to as a 'bent arm' pull or 'S' pull.

In the 'S' pull, after entry the hand should move smoothly downwards and outwards to gain a firm fix on the water just below the surface. This action will be assisted by the roll of the shoulder towards the pulling arm. Your hand should now continue to move downwards and outwards in a circular path. As your hand comes in line with your head, your elbow should begin to flex and the hand should move upwards and inwards towards the surface. At this

Rica Reinisch (East Germany) winning 100m backstroke at the 1980 Moscow Olympics with a new world record

point your arm will be in line with your shoulder, with the elbow flexed around 90 degrees and the tips of your fingers just under the surface pointing upwards and outwards. It is important to remember that if you have not rolled sufficiently, then your hand may break the surface of the water. The final part of this arm movement is a downwards push towards the thigh. The movement should be an accelerated one, with the hand finishing below the hip and a strong push towards the bottom of the pool.

The recovery of the arm action for both underwater styles is similar in that it should be made with a high, relaxed and straight arm which will move over the water in a vertical path. As the arm passes over the shoulder, it should rotate so that the hand is ready to enter, little finger first.

BACK CRAWL

1. *The left arm is just entering the water, the hand below the surface and the little finger leading. The right hand is preparing to leave the water, leading the right arm into its recovery phase. Note the left hand aligned along the centre line of the body.*

2. *After entry the left hand moves, palm downwards and fingers leading, to catch point.*

3. *The elbow bends and drops throughout the pull phase, and the hand moves upwards and inwards as it comes towards the surface. At the point where the hand is opposite the shoulder, the elbow is bent to approximately 90°, whilst the tips of the fingers are just under the surface, pointing upwards and outwards.*

(BENT ARM)

LEGS

As for front crawl: with minimal bending at the knee and ankles and feet stretched, the legs alternately kick throughout the sequence. The feet pass close to each other in the in-toed position.

4. The left hand moves beyond the point of the shoulder into the push phase. It leads the elbow as it extends towards the hip with a strong accelerating movement downwards before the right rotates to allow the hand to exit palm inwards, thumb first. The right arm is in the final stages of recovery.

5. Sequence begins again with right arm.

BACK CRAWL TURN SEQUENCE

1. *The leading hand, close to the body's midline, reaches for the wall with fingers pointing downwards. The arm should be slightly bent so that its subsequent extension helps push the body round. Note the trailing hand is pushing upwards to assist with the rotational spin as the knees begin to bend.*

2. *Knees and hips flex and spin towards the leading hand. Both hands are beginning to move back towards the head.*

3. *The body rotates to enable the feet to plant firmly on the wall, knees slightly flexed for greater force in the subsequent extension. The hands now move away from the head as the body begins to stretch out for the push-off.*

4. *The swimmer is in a fully extended glide position on her back during the vigorous push-off. The legs resume their alternating kick, and the first arm stroke starts: the body is thus returned to the surface.*

LEG ACTION

The leg kick which you should practise for back crawl is very similar to the front crawl kick described in the previous section. The leg's movement is similar to kicking a football. It is essential in back crawl to have a strong, effective kick, as this will assist in obtaining and maintaining a good stable body position. We can look at the leg action in two parts – a strong upward beat and a downward movement. In order to achieve this strong upbeat, the kick should be initiated from the hip. The upper leg will start to rise, while the lower leg continues to drop to its lowest point. As the upper leg continues to rise to the surface the lower leg should follow in a strong whip action until the toes dimple the surface of the water. This whip movement will be more effective if you can perform it with an in-toeing action and relaxed flexible ankles. The downward beat is not a strong propulsive movement and you should aim to drop the leg downwards from the hips while keeping the leg relatively straight.

One of the common problems seen in inexperienced back crawl swimmers is that of a cycling action. Although some flexion in the knee is necessary, it is essential that the movement is initiated from the hips, therefore excessive knee flexion should be avoided.

Breathing is not a difficult thing to achieve in back crawl, but initially problems occur through your having an irregular breathing pattern. You should try to develop a rhythm in your breathing by breathing in as one arm enters the water and breathing out as the other arm enters.

GETTING IT TOGETHER

Finally, let us consider the timing, or coordination, of the stroke. You should be aiming for a continuous stroke with no pause. The arm action should be accompanied by six beats to every one arm cycle; therefore, as the right arm enters the water the left leg kicks up, and as the left arm enters so the right leg kicks up.

Now to summarize the points we should be looking for in a well-performed back crawl stroke. You should aim for a high body position, with the hips and head still. An effective arm action should be developed and this will be made easier with the introduction of body roll into your stroke. Finally a well-practised leg action which is continuous and has a strong upward movement, together with good coordination and a rhythmic breathing pattern, will all go towards a good stroke.

CLIFF DEDYNSKI

Breaststroke

THE BREASTSTROKE CONTROVERSY

For many years now breaststroke has been one of the most controversial strokes. You may think of it as a slow and disjointed way to move through the water, or you may find it a relaxing and very natural movement. Certainly most of my swimmers tend either to love or hate this particular stroke. Its action is disputed even amongst the national and international bodies which control competitive swimming. When you are swimming breaststroke, for example, should your head always be above the water or are you allowed to dip under occasionally? When executing a turn must you hit the wall with shoulders parallel to the water's surface, or are you allowed to touch the wall lopsided? So, given such controversy, how should you be swimming breaststroke? Well, the kick is a good place to start.

Before looking at the drills, for kicking, there are two points to bear in mind. First,

do not concentrate so hard on your legs that you forget about arms, timing or body position. Admittedly some world-class breaststrokers rely heavily on a very powerful leg kick, but others rely just as heavily on their arms and shoulders. Second, breaststroke kicking can subject your knees to unusual stresses, therefore injury to the knees is a real possibility. You can avoid such injuries by adopting a 'softly-softly' approach. For example, I never let my swimmers sprint, or go really fast on breaststroke until they have warmed up thoroughly. It is a good idea to spend your first ten of fifteen minutes in the water either on other strokes – such as front crawl – or if you prefer, swimming a much more relaxed style of breaststroke, gradually stretching and kicking a little harder as your joints and muscles get warmed up.

Cliff Dedynski has a background in law and education. He is an ASA teacher and coach, a member of the ASA Coaching Education sub-committee, and currently holds the position of Chief Coach to Oundle and District Swim Squad

(Opposite) Steve Lundquist (USA), gold medallist for 100m breaststroke at the 1984 Los Angeles Olympics

KICKING DRILLS

One of my favourite drills involves using a front crawl arm action. This mixed-up stroke is very similar to that known as the 'trudgeon', which was the fastest known stroke many years ago. The advantage of this exercise is that it takes the pressure off your arms and, therefore, allows you to concentrate on your kick.

Another popular drill which helps you to see what your legs are doing involves swimming on your back. Your legs must kick in breaststroke fashion and you can actually watch your own knees – and, less easily, your feet – to make sure that they are doing the right thing. When doing this you can just scull with your hands by your sides, use an alternating back crawl arm action, or take both arms up and over at the same time. I have a preference for the last method. Technically it is referred to as the 'Old English' backstroke, and it is very popular amongst my better swimmers. If you float well, or have a strong breast-stroke kick, it is probably ideal for you. On the other hand, if you have a weak breast-stroke, I would advise you to use the first of the arm actions, sculling with your arms by your sides.

IS YOUR KICK IN GOOD SHAPE?

Although the exercises that we have just considered will help to improve your breaststroke, they will be even more helpful if you know *how* your feet and knees should be propelling you through the water. At this stage, I usually talk about Charlie Chaplin. Most of us have seen his famous walk, with feet turned right out. All good breaststrokers have the ability to turn their feet outwards in this way. The feet are used rather like a pair of paddles but the kick should, in fact, be circular. I usually tell my swimmers to kick backwards, out and around, bringing the feet together at the end of the kick. This may sound easy, but if a swimmer struggles to turn the feet outwards just as they reach their bottom, then there will be little propulsion from the kick. Another point to work on here is the speed of the kick. You should not simply kick your feet backwards, out, around and together all at the same speed. There is more acceleration in the breaststroke kick than in any of the other kicks. I usually explain this by saying that as your legs finish sweeping outwards and start to sweep inwards, then you must accelerate the kick: Speed up your feet as they kick around the corner.

USING YOUR KNEES – AN OPEN AND CLOSED CASE!

Not so long ago, I remember everyone being told to 'kick like a frog'. For most people this conjured up images of keeping their knees wide apart as they brought their feet towards their bottoms. If you use this style, then your knees and feet form a wedge-shape and you have a wedge-kick. It is by far the most common of breaststroke kicks and is ideal for relaxed, easy recreational breaststroke swimming; it also has the advantage of putting less pressure on the sides of your knees. On the other hand, I must admit that I enjoy coaching a rather different kick which involves keeping your knees fairly close together and allowing your feet to separate just before they kick backwards. This particular style is known as the 'whip-kick' and is now used by most top-class breaststrokers. Without a doubt, this style of kick subjects your knees to greater stresses than the traditional wedge-kick. You must be careful not to rush into the whip-kick until you have spent plenty of time warming up, and perhaps more time on the wedge-kick before you switch to the whip-kick.

BREAST STROKE

1. The swimmer's arms are at full stretch at the end of a recovery phase. The legs are in the process of kicking outwards and backwards to complete their vigorous accelerating drive, with the feet beginning to rotate inwards. The face is about to enter the water after breathing.

2. The palms are rotating as they move outwards and backwards towards catch point. The legs come towards each other with the inward foot rotation continuing.

3. The hands move through catch and into pull phase with the elbows beginning to bend into a more efficient angle. The legs are now fully extended and in a streamlined position.

USING YOUR KNEES

There is one final point with regard to your knee action. I have seen many aspiring breaststrokers bringing their knees too far forward – almost to their chest – and then kicking with all their strength, only to find that they almost stop dead each time. There is no magic formula here, but it is a good idea to experiment by bringing your knees forward a little less. Try several different knee positions until you feel the most comfortable.

4. The arms continue through the pull phase, elbows still bending and hands assuming a typical paddle-like effect: their action pulls the body forwards and upwards and causes the head to surface for breathing. The legs begin recovery prior to the next propulsive phase.

5. The hands have completed the propulsive pull phase and have moved inwards smoothly and rapidly. They begin their recovery, moving forward to full stretch. The head is still clear of the water for the breathing action. The legs are about to drive back, starting the sequence over again.

WHAT ABOUT YOUR ARMS?

A number of swimmers and coaches are inclined to neglect the arm action. This is a pity, especially when taking into account the fact that many top class breaststrokers can 'pull' an all-out 50 metre breaststroke at least as quickly as they can 'kick' an all-out 50.

So, how should you be using your arms and shoulders? In the first place, your hands should move in a circular fashion and, just as your legs must accelerate throughout each kick, so too must your hands and arms accelerate (from a mere 2ft per second to approximately 20ft per second). Apart from such acceleration, I tend to work hard on keeping a high elbow position during the first half of the pull. Nearly all swimmers, including good breaststrokers, are prone to collapse their elbows too early. This is a bad habit to get into and definitely slows you down. I emphasize that the elbows should not be allowed to drop until the hands have virtually come together ready for the recovery to begin. Although it may sound easy, I have to spend a lot of time on this point, especially as swimmers begin to get tired. It is also important to keep altering the pitch of your hands. As you develop a 'feel' for the water, so you should become accustomed to changing the pitch of your hands from an 'outward and downward' movement during the outsweep of the arms to an 'inward and upward' movement at the end of the insweep. Practise this every time you swim breaststroke and don't be afraid to experiment a little with your hand pitch.

One final point is the position of your shoulders relative to the water-level, which is now one of the most controversial aspects of modern breaststroke swimming. Should you stay *flat* in the water with your shoulders almost always submerged, or should you lift your shoulders well clear of the water as your hands pull in and you take a breath? There is no general consensus on this, but I prefer a compromise situation and therefore explain to my swimmers that they should lift their shoulders up and forward a little as their hands pull together. I tell them to lean forward slightly as they breathe, but to make sure that they keep most of the chest in the water.

BREAST STROKE TURN

1. Both hands touch the wall simultaneously, the shoulders remaining in the horizontal plane (ASA laws). The flexion at the elbows allows for a forceful push from the wall. This will assist the subsequent swinging movement of the knees and hips.

4. Feet are planted on the wall, knees bent. Arms stretch in readiness for a full glide position: the body is now on its side.

2. The hands push off: the hips and knees rotate in readiness for the leg extension.

3. The legs stretch towards the wall, and the hands away from the head. The body starts rotating to a side position.

5. Legs extend and drive away from the wall. The swimmer rotates her body so that as her feet leave the wall, she is on her front (ASA laws).

Note: following the glide the arms will push/pull through to the hips with high elbows, as in the powerful pull/push phase of the butterfly stroke. After recovery, the next arm action must take place at the surface of the water (ASA laws).

GETTING IT TOGETHER

It seems strange that you can have a strong kick, an efficient pull and yet a poor over-all breaststroke. The problem, of course, is one of coordination and timing. If you swim breaststroke for fun and relaxation, then you will probably have a marked 'gliding' phase. This is perfectly all right, and usually comes at the end of the kick and just before you start your next pull. In competitive swimming, however, there should be no gliding phase at all. If you are gliding, you probably have a 'dead-spot' in your stroke where you are slowing down. Consequently, I coach what is technically called 'continuous' timing or, in cases where the kick is very weak, 'overlap' timing. If you have a balanced stroke with equally strong kick and pull, then you should start pulling just as the legs finish their kick. If your kick is somewhat on the weak side, then you should start pulling just before your kick finishes. This ensures smooth, continuous movement through the water.

Finally, back to the breathing and turning controversy mentioned at the beginning of this section. Currently your head must break the general water level once each stroke cycle except at the turns, where you are allowed to dip under and do one underwater armstroke as you push away from the wall. A couple of years ago, several international swimmers were disqualified for submerging their heads. It is an easy trap to fall into if you either deliberately swim a little slowly, conserving energy for a 'final', or if you use a lot of butterfly-type movement. As for the turns the touch must be made with both hands simultaneously, and the shoulders must remain in the horizontal plane.

Learning to swim – the fundamentals

DAVID HICKS

Butterfly

A NEW STROKE IS BORN

The butterfly stroke is the newest of the four recognized competitive swimming strokes. It came into being as the result of breaststroke being swum in all kinds of different ways, culminating in an arm recovery over the water which gave a greater advantage than underwater recovery. In 1952 the butterfly stroke – as a competitive event with its own set of rules – was born. Meantime, the laws on breaststroke were tightened up and little change has taken place since then.

Certain bogeys have dogged the butterfly stroke over the years, such as teachers being over-cautious in introducing it as part of a multistroke method of teaching, or being afraid to let children attempt it, thinking that it is necessary to be very strong and aggressive in order to perform it. While I agree that strength is indeed important, and a certain amount of aggres-sion is essential, surely these are required on every stroke in these modern times? I believe technique is the key factor in getting to grips with what might be called this most prestigious of strokes. Once a swimmer can perform butterfly stroke, in terms of swimming prowess, they have arrived! In any pool you will see swimmers doing front crawl, back crawl and breaststroke, but how often do you see butterfly in a recreational swimming session? Even in a swimming club situation, there are hundreds of swimmers using the other three strokes, but look for the first stroke 'fliers' and they are few and far between. Taking this into account, it should be easier to achieve success in the butterfly than in any other stroke, but try to convince swimmers of this! So, let us start with the position of the body, because it is from this platform that everything takes shape.

(Opposite) Michael Gross (West Germany), currently recognized as the finest swimmer in the west because of his wide abilities. 1984 Olympic gold medallist 200m freestyle, 100m butterfly; 1985 European gold medallist, 200m and 100m butterfly; 1986 world champion 200m freestyle, 200m butterfly.

David Hicks is ASA National Development Officer, Crystal Palace National Sports Centre

65

BODY POSITION

I like to see the body as flat as possible in the water, but allowing for the leg kick. Undulation of the body will take place during the stroke-cycle, caused by the reaction of the arm and leg movements and the raising of the head for breathing. The downward kick of the legs raises the hips upwards, while the arms tend to raise the head and shoulders. Arm recovery over the water will drop the hips; this then causes undulation, which must be kept to a minimum. Flexibility helps to maintain a flat body position, as will breath-holding. Keeping the head low on breathing will help. I like to see the chin pushed forward – making a furrow in the water to breathe – rather than a definite head lift. This is naturally good for streamlining and allows for maximum oxygen intake in the minimum of time as the air passage is in a straight line. I have already mentioned the important fact that the leg kick helps to keep the body flat, but a certain amount of propulsion can also be gained from the kicking action, always provided that this is efficient. Most good butterfly swimmers look for some propulsion during the non-propulsive phase – that is, during recovery.

THE LEGS

During the leg kick, both feet kick downwards with ankles extended, to a depth of maybe 50 cm (20 in) to 60 cm (24 in). The resulting up-thrust causes the hips to rise as the legs are fully extended. The legs, while fully stretched, start to rise with the soles of the feet, creating an upward and backward force on the water. The hips will now start to drop once again, leading the upper legs in a downwards movement with the knees bending, while the lower legs and feet continue to rise. This action continues until the knees bend quite considerably and the ankles are fully extended. The lower legs then start the propulsive thrust downwards, with flexible ankles and with a whip-like action. The hips will then rise and the complete cycle will begin all over again. It must be remembered that both legs work together; this is dictated by the laws of the stroke, that there must be no alternating movement of the feet. It is known as 'dolphin' leg action and it balances the body throughout the stroke cycle.

(Opposite) Butterfly action: note the breathing action as head and shoulders emerge from the water, followed by the arms in their over-water recovery phase. The head then begins to drop back in the water.

BUTTERFLY

1. The arm position is just after entry, thumbs first, having completed the out of water recovery. The legs are just finishing their first (major) downwards and backwards beat, coinciding with the entry of the arms.

2. The arms begin the pull phase, moving towards catch point.

3. The arms are now well into the pull phase, with the elbows high and the hands travelling palm first and paddle-like towards the feet. The legs are in recovery position.

Side view of picture 2.

4. *The hands have come closer together below the shoulders and are now beginning the push phase. The legs begin their second (minor) downward beat.*

5. *The arms are well into the push phase.*

6. *The arms have travelled backwards and are reaching the end of the pull phase. Palms are beginning to rotate inwards so that exit from the water will occur, elbows first, with little fingers leading the hand. The legs are reaching the furthest point of their second (minor) downwards beat.*

Side view of picture 5.

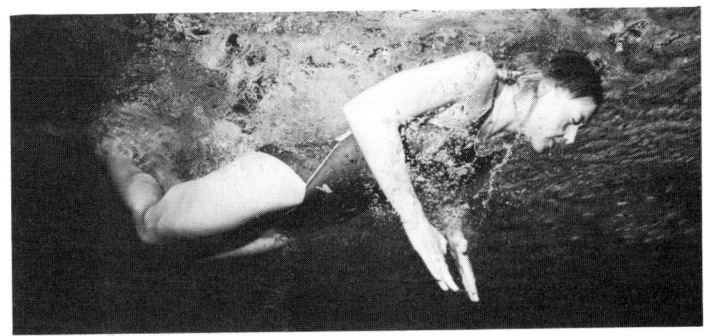

7. *The arms are now swung upwards and round through recovery. The legs begin recovery*

8. *The arms are moving towards the entry point. The legs are about to kick down on the next downward (major) beat to coincide with the arm entry and move to catch point. The cycle begins again.*

BUTTERFLY TURN

Look back to the pictures illustrating the breast stroke turn on pages 60–1. The two-handed touch in picture 1 and the subsequent movements in pictures 2, 3, 4 and 5 are very similar to those for the butterfly turn. The two strokes differ at the push off: the breast stroke swimmer's glide tends to be deeper than that of the butterfly swimmer, who makes a shorter, energetic, shallow glide before returning to the surface with the commencement of the kick. This is followed by the first arm action.

THE ARMS

The arm action is the major source of propulsion in a stroke where strength and mobility of the shoulders is most important. The arms must move simultaneously (to comply with the laws) and continuously. The hands enter the water in front of or just outside the shoulder line. This will depend on the amount of mobility in the shoulder girdle. Once in the 'catch' position about 15 cm (6 in) to 20 cm (8 in) under the surface of the water, the palms of the hands should fix on the water facing the direction of the pull – that is, towards the feet. I like to see a thumbs-first entry, as this helps to hold the elbow in a high position, allowing more area to come in contact with pressure of the pull. A weak swimmer will tend to hold on in the catch position, causing a long pause and using his legs. Try not to develop this, as it will become a habit and spoil the continuity of the stroke. It is during the pull-push phase that the power is turned on. Hand and wrist remain firm, with the palms of the hands facing towards the feet throughout. From the catch position, the hands pull downwards, backwards, and then sideways. The arms bend when the hands are 30 cm (12 in) to 45 cm (18 in) deep and the hands move towards one another under the chest, in a curved pathway. As the body moves forward, emphasis is placed on the powerful backward push of the hands as they continue this movement, ending at the thighs ready for recovery. We call this pattern an hourglass shape, or keyhole. During the recovery the elbows leave the water first, with the palms facing upwards although some swimmers have palms facing inwards. The hands are carried sideways and forwards in a smooth relaxed flinging action. As the arms pass the shoulders, the hands face downwards, then extend forwards in front of the shoulders, ready for entry to start the arm cycle once again. During the recovery the laws of the stroke state that the arms must clear the water and not be pushed through it.

BREATHING

Breathing in the butterfly stroke is critical, because the raising of the upper body to bring the mouth clear of the water level causes undulation. Breathing takes place at the end of the push phase as the arms come up into the recovery position, but the head and shoulders begin to rise much earlier – that is, in the pull phase. At this stage the chin leads the way, making a furrow in the water. I like to see the swimmer keeping low in the water to prevent too much resistance. The breath is taken quickly, then the head is lowered for a streamlined body position as the hands recover for the entry in front of the shoulder. Explosive breathing, the blow-stuck action, is favoured as this helps to maintain more buoyancy. Fitness will influence whether breathing should take place every stroke or every other stroke. Most fit competitive swimmers will breathe every two strokes for efficiency and speed. Some swimmers breathe to the side, but this may well cause problems as breathing is restricted; there is then a tendency to drop the shoulders on the non-breathing side and thus contravene the laws of the stroke. The body must be on the breast, with the shoulders horizontal from the beginning of the first arm stroke after the start and after the turn. I like to see the swimmer breathe to the front.

GETTING IT ALL TOGETHER

Coordination of this stroke normally means that there are two leg kicks per arm cycle. A major kick comes as the hands start the pull at the catch position, because at this stage the hips have dropped due to the arms recovering over the water, and the head has lifted for breathing. A secondary kick takes place at the end of the push as the head and shoulders begin to rise, because the hips are dropping once again. There are variations as to how many kicks and how vigorous or otherwise they should be, but normally we speak of a major/minor kick.

LEARNING THE STROKE

When starting to teach the butterfly stroke, I like to begin slowly over short distances. What is the point of pressurizing an unstable stroke? Push and glide practices into and from the side are essential for all strokes. We can add a dolphin leg kick, emphasizing that both legs must work together with no alternating or crawl leg action. Static practices at the rail should only be used sparingly. You should use a float, arms extended to the front, kicking widths or even half-widths to get the rhythm going. Try the arm action in the water, bending forward with stable legs on the bottom of the pool. Practise the arm movements, then transfer to full stroke doing dolphin leg kicks and then one arm-throw. Continue this, but add two arm actions, with no breathing at this stage.

Once a pattern begins to develop, then kick, kick, kick, throw, kick, kick and stop. Work slowly developing a good body position, then increase to a width, maybe adding a breath – then two. It is a bad teacher or coach who will try to rush this stroke, giving rise to bad habits and poor stroke technique. Many teachers use a breaststroke leg kick with the over water recovery for beginners. I can see the logic in this, but it also means that eventually the swimmer will have to re-learn the dolphin kick as this is the fastest combination. Butterfly arms with breaststroke legs is quite legal, but this means that it is a slower stroke rate as the timing is now dictated by the legs, not the arms. Recovery of the legs in breaststroke is slow because of the resistance on drawing up

72

the legs. Once the semblance of a good stroke is established, practise regularly over short distances. If you find you cannot get your arms clear of the water on recovery in training – stop. Rest, then make another attempt.

For competitive swimmers, I prefer to see 'legs only' practices in dolphin, carried out within the use of a float. This is not so restricting to upper-body movement, and places less pressure on the lower areas of the spine. Medical research, particularly in Britain, has been undertaken to study the effects of such stress on the back; caution must be observed.

What a lovely sight it is to see a good butterfly swimmer in action: controlled aggression and power. I have seen many wonderful swimmers of this majestic stroke, but my favourite is still Mark Spitz, even though this dates me somewhat. When you realize how much flexibility, power and strength are needed to execute this stroke effectively, you appreciate how hard you have to train to get anywhere near the top; but what an achievement when you get there!

Mark Spitz (USA), one of the greatest all-round swimmers of all time. At the 1972 Olympic Games he broke seven world records and won seven gold medals, including this butterfly event.

CHARLES WILSON

Individual Medley

INTRODUCTION

'Look, Dad, what I can do!' The simple swim across the width was nothing more than a few front crawl strokes and a bit of back crawl. This change from stroke to stroke is one of the earliest and obviously enjoyable water games.

As kids we raced across the pool on 'front-back overarm' long before we heard of individual medley; one arm doing front crawl, the other arm back crawl, cheating as much as we dared in order to win – it was fun. Strict stroke order, laws and specialist methods of training there may be, but if the infinite variety of your personal, unique mixture of swimming movements is forgotten you will lose more than half the fun, the variety and the benefits of the 'IM'; and this applies as much to the world's top swimmers as it does to the beginner in armbands. The space of one section does not permit the inclusion of all that can be said about the 'fifth stroke', therefore it will only consider the individual medley as defined in the rule book, but do not forget that there is a whole range of athletic swimming movements outside the rules as we know them – drills and skills which can be strung together to provide competition the rule-makers never dreamt about. Medleys improve training enjoyment with a variety which taxes the imagination, challenges skill and ability and develops endurance.

THE COMPETITIVE EVENTS

Butterfly, backstroke, breaststroke, freestyle – this has been laid down as the stroke order, with the ruling that freestyle may not be one of the other strokes. Each stroke is subject to the laws of that stroke

Charles Wilson is an ASA Senior Coach and Staff Tutor, Technical Director to the Institute of Swimming Teachers and Coaches, a founder member and past president of the British Swimming Coaches Association and a GB and Olympic team coach

Sarah Hardcastle, during the breaststroke leg of the 400m individual medley in the 1986 Commonwealth Games – she won the bronze. Sarah also holds, amongst other awards, 1984 Olympic 400m freestyle silver, 1986 World Championships 400m freestyle bronze, 1986 Commonwealth Championships 800 freestyle gold, 400m freestyle gold

from the beginning to the completion of each distance. Strokes must be swum in four sections of equal distance.

As a recognized competition event, it began as three strokes until butterfly became an event in its own right in 1953. As a 300 yards/metre event the records go back to 1922, when Hilda James swam a 300-yard medley in 4 mins 40 secs. It was always a popular local event, often swum as a novelty with the stroke order back-stroke, breaststroke, freestyle. There are even stories that a four-stroke medley was swum pre-1930 by Rademacher, who was adept at two types of breaststroke – with and without an over-water recovery. The event settled down as a four-stroke event after 1953, but it was not until 1964 that the 400-metre medley became an Olympic

event with the 200-metre medley following in 1968. The 200-metre event was dropped as an Olympic event in 1972 and reinstated in 1984. Those who watch the trends and have imagination are speculating that, with the ever-increasing use of electronic timing at club level and the subsequent gain in popularity of true sprint events, the 100-metre individual medley will become an accepted short-course event. The sprint/power requirement and the high degree of stroke and turning skill will make it truly exciting. The full history of the 'IM' is as interesting and as varied as the event itself. The story that the event's inclusion was delayed because the post-lunch announcer found 'individual medley' beyond the tongue's range is almost certainly untrue!

THE LONG AND SHORT MEDLEYS, 400 AND 200 METRES

Participation in these events depends almost entirely on age and type of swimmer – sprint or endurance. For the younger age-group swimmer the 200-metre medley, particularly long course (i.e. events swum in a 50-metre pool rather than a 25-metre pool), has very little sprint component. The event only becomes a sprint in late age-grouping and senior

swimming (16+ boys, 14+ girls), and reverts to the ranks of endurance events for the middle-aged masters' swimmer. This is certainly a cry for the introduction of the 100-metre medley as an official event. The 400-metre medley, a tough power/endurance event, has no place in young age-group or masters' swimming.

SHORT COURSE AND LONG COURSE?

The long-course or short-course factor throws in yet another consideration as to how a swimmer develops the individual

medley. Strictly speaking, with the exception of 50-metre races, there are no true sprints in 50-metre pools. Endurance is always a major factor in long-course swimming, but not so great in short-course pools. It is the extra endurance factor in long-course swimming which makes swimming medley in short pools an important development step before competing in the long-course equivalent. Individual medleys are far more demanding swum in 50-metre pools. Short-course or long-course, for the fully-fledged swimmer the 200-metre medley should be looked upon as a sprint or, more accurately, four 50-metre sprints. Having said that, it must still be remembered that the total event is 200 metres and, therefore, there is an endurance factor. Training should contain a large sprint element. Skill, power and sheer vigour are important attributes of the short medley swimmer. For those looking for future 400-metre medley swimmers, one of the best guides is the ability to compete on a short medley rather than 100-metre or 200-metre ability on separate strokes. It seems that the ability to maintain good form when changing from stroke to stroke is very important.

THE 400-METRE IM

As a competitive event, the 'long medley' is the most interesting and the most demanding of all races; it is the conductor of the orchestra of swimming competition and should form the basis of every general club training programme. It provides a training aim second to none because:

—it offers immense variety
—it provides the widest possible all-round physical development
—it motivates multi-skill acquisition
—it develops mental attributes of care, thought, toughness and the intellectual capability of the real champion
—it is the perfect event for those who have no outstanding specific stroke ability, but who can aspire to quality in all strokes and ARE PREPARED TO WORK HARD
—in practical terms it is an event in which you can achieve status because, for many reasons, few swimmers specialize in it

General indicators in racing the long medley are:
—consideration of splits is all-important. Swimmer and coach must study and analyse these
—all-round ability is essential. The one-stroke-strength (particularly on breaststroke) medley swimmer still figures in races even at national level, but it is clear that at world level quality ALL-ROUND ability is vital
—self-knowledge and confidence is important
—mental race pressures have an important role (see 'classic race')
—at all levels, but chiefly with inexperienced competitors, there is a distinct danger of swimmers relaxing effort on their weak strokes in order to reserve energy for the strong.

We shall look at these factors more closely when we come to training for the medley.

The classic 400-metre IM race of all time was the final of the men's event in the 1972 Olympic Games, won by Gunnar Larsson of Sweden from Tim McKee of USA by $\frac{1}{1000}$ of a second. After this race FINA (the international governing body of swimming) changed the law of timing; times henceforth would be to hundredths of a second rather than thousandths. McKee can consider himself unlucky not to have a gold medal in his showcase.

This race exemplified all the above-mentioned indicators in just over four and a half minutes. The splits chart of the race explains how certain swimmers had considered their strengths and weaknesses. Larsson knew of his ability over the second half; Hall was aware of his first-half superiority; McKee, Hargittay and Furniss were confident of their all-round ability. What cannot be seen on this race alone is the thought and 'split' consideration put into Windeatt's race preparation; he improved 16 seconds from 1970 to 1972. Comparing this race – only the third in Olympic history – with that of 1984, the development toward equal all-stroke ability is clear. Larsson's knowledge of his own weaknesses almost overstepped the boundary and it required extreme self-confidence and mental toughness to be so far down at half-way, only to come back as he did to win. He swam his own race and won. The mental pressure on Hall, who knew that his strengths were in butterfly and backstroke, was the cause of his over-emphasis on that part of the race at the cost of the second half. McKee and Furniss were tough and mentally aware in rising to the occasion and in sticking to a race pattern. Hargitty, the second favourite and certainly the man with the all-round talent and experience, failed to meet the occasion.

Examination of those splits can tell you more; it was a classic.

An excellent example of the mental alertness required comes from more recent history. Ray Terrell was the outstanding IM swimmer of Great Britain and full of confidence, maybe over-confidence. He was faced by a wily young campaigner called Martyn Woodroffe. Terrell knew Woodroffe had the advantage on 'fly, but was not God's gift to backstroke. Terrell, however, was an acknowledged backstroker. Terrell 'gave' Woodroffe the 'fly, but relaxed too much mentally as well as physically, supremely confident that he would take the backstroke. Woodroffe turned from fly to back like a flash and rocketed off on backstroke. Terrell loafed his turn somewhat, pushed off and glanced sideways expecting to see Woodroffe's feet, but even the bubbles had disappeared. Shock and another look round lost more time, then realization of what had happened took further toll and Woodroffe had won.

Any swimmer or coach who hopes for success at world level in the 400-metre IM should expect to become something of a historian in the sport. This is a race of infinite variety; the more that can be experienced from the past, the greater will be the success, and the less likelihood of being defeated mentally.

Gunnar Larsson, gold medallist in the 1972 Olympic Games Individual Medley 400m. The butterfly leg of the race

Tim McKee during the backstroke leg of the same race. He came second, losing the race by one-thousandth of a second

THE CLASSIC – MUNICH 1972

	BUTTERFLY	BACKSTROKE	BREASTSTROKE	FREESTYLE
Larsson	1:03.41 63.41	2:14.67 70.66	3:32.17 77.50	4:31.98 59.81
McKee	1:02.06 62.06	2:10.66 68.60	3:29.91 79.25	4:31.98 62.07
Hargittay	1:00.22 . 60.22	2:10.80 70.58	3:31.62 80.82	4:32.70 60.45
Furniss	1:00.78 67.78	2:10.09 69.31	3:32.88 82.79	4:35.44 62.56
Hall	58.38 58.38	2:06.32 67.94	3:31.04 85.72	4:37.38 66.34
Ljunberg	1:01.05 61.65	2:11.15 70.10	3:36.11 84.96	4:37.96 61.85
Windeatt	1:03.70 63.70	2:15.87 72.17	3:38.76 82.89	4:40.39 62.63
Sperberg	1:03.80 63.80	2:15.76 71.96	3:36.38 78.62	4:40.66 64.28
Terrell	1:01.80 61.80	2:12.40 70.60	3:38.50 86.10	4:42.70 64.20

DEVELOPMENT & TRAINING FOR COMPETITION

1 Planning and careful monitoring of training sessions is vital to achieve an essential balance so that nothing is over-looked. Multiply by four all the factors you need to train on one stroke; add changes of rhythm, variation of turning, the need for power, endurance, sprint ability and flexibility. You will then see the necessity for planning.

2 It is essential to race on ALL strokes separately, including the weakest and least favourite. IT IS VERY IMPORTANT TO RACE ON THE WEAKEST OR LEAST FAVOURITE STROKES.

3 Early in the year, develop each stroke on a cyclic basis. Some prefer, for example, to work on a different stroke each day in a constant cycle, whereas others prefer an *emphasis* on a particular stroke each day, but including all strokes.

4 After two months, begin to put the strokes together, gradually linking the total medley.

It is at this stage that the true variety of the event will be clear. The most obvious is the two- or three-stroke combinations, butterfly to backstroke, backstroke to breaststroke and breaststroke to freestyle, or linking three strokes. The distance on each stroke can be varied. At the earliest stage of this build-up period the weaker strokes, or the two power strokes ('fly and breaststroke), should be swum with shorter distances than the back and free. Built up in this way, correct pace can be achieved from the beginning. For example, in the first week a combination swim could be 25-metre 'fly, 75-metre backstroke, leading to 50-metre/75-metre then 75-metre/75-metre, 75-metre/100-metre and finally 100-metre 'fly, 100-metre backstroke for a 200-metre combination. Another way of achieving build-up is to combine drills with drills, or drills and full stroke, such as 25-metre 'fly, 100-metre dolphin kick, 100-metre backstroke.

Obviously imagination is essential, at the same time as a thorough knowledge of the physiological demands and of stroke mechanics – also how these can serve you or be served by the medley.

5 At the linking stage full medleys should be swum in training and competition to discover individual strengths and problems.

6 The number of repetitions and the time aims depend upon the qualities of the swimmer.

7 A part of training to develop the mental toughness and fitness is 'negative split-ting', i.e. swimming the second half of a particular stroke/distance faster than the first half. Negative split 200-metre swims on all strokes are essential in the development of a 400-metre IM swimmer.

8 Turns are a vital part of training at all times, but as a major event approaches greater concentration on turns is excellent for the mental approach to competition.

It may help to stimulate the imagination if the coach can think in terms of varying **skills (drills), distance, resting times, number of repetitions, lap times** and **overall time spent on aspects of training** when planning training for the IM events.

INDIVIDUAL MEDLEY AS AN AID TO DEVELOPMENT AND GENERAL TRAINING

All young swimmers should regard the individual medley as their main stroke; it is essential in skill development. In answer to the telephone call from a 'new' parent telling me that his 12-year-old son was a backstroker, the answer was, 'We have no 12-year-old backstrokers, only 12-year-old swimmers.' Young children should be multiSPORT developed, and within the sport of swimming MULTISTROKE should be part of the development. The natural outcome of this is the individual medley. If competitions for young swimmers were widened to include combination events culminating in the individual medley, we would certainly witness an improvement in our junior swimming, a greater depth in quality and far less early retirement. The use of various forms of medley is a first-class method of building and developing endurance and for the same reason is a form of over-distance training.

IM is an excellent way of building distance into an early season programme, increasing variety and reducing the possibility of over-use injury which can be a problem, particularly with breaststroke swimmers, early in the season. It is very sound advice to breaststroke swimmers to begin their year's programme with individual medley swimming. For the sake of variety in a training programme, medley swimming is a 'must'. The possibilities opened up by combining strokes and drills are virtually limitless when you consider all the strokes, the part strokes, the drills, kicking, pulling, synchro and water polo skills which can be combined to make up medleys for any effect desired.

One of the problems of masters' swimming, particularly for the middle-aged and older age swimmer, could easily be over-use injuries. Again, medleys can help achieve distance and fitness, not just the 'individual medley' but also medleys involving sidestroke, life-saving backstroke and sculling. Once more we return to that word 'imagination'. Laws of sport are essential, true, but they must not be restrictive. There has been a tendency in sport to see training and development within very narrow limits imposed by these laws, and this is detrimental in every aspect – participation, teaching, coaching and administration. Forget the rules, allow the imagination to develop, and use individual medley in its widest sense. Children lack the experience and knowledge to do this for themselves – an opportunity to develop medley swimming lies in masters' swimming.

TONY MACKENZIE-FARMER

Part Two: Everybody can swim – it's fun

PARENT AND BABY WATER ACTIVITIES

European children who live in hot climates invariably swim well at an early age, due to the warm water and warmer surroundings. In this country, a warm swimming pool simplifies the task of learning to swim. As very young babies cannot maintain their body temperature in cold water, it is worth travelling far afield to find a pool that is warm.

Start at home in the baby bath with very young babies, then progress to the full-size bath and finally to the public pool. I do not think it wise to do as shown on some films and to carry out swimming experiments with babies when they are first born. However, even the new-born baby can enjoy bathtime, and parents can further their baby's watermanship right from the start.

Ensure that the water in the baby bath is 'elbow' warm and that the air temperature

Tony MacKenzie-Farmer MA, has a very wide experience in teaching at all levels, both in UK and abroad. He is an ASA Staff Tutor and has a particular interest in parent and baby swimming.

is a little warmer. Have towels ready for drying afterwards. Support the baby (especially the head), keeping the body immersed. Whilst crooning or talking to the baby, rock it gently, head first and then feet first, without the ripples covering the baby's head. If the baby enjoys this, tentatively find out his reaction to water on his hair and running down his face. I do this by pouring water from my hand onto his head. Babies under approximately three months old have a reflex that keeps water out of their lungs, but older babies will have lost this reflex and may show some distress. In this situation, persevere slowly so that the baby gradually becomes familiar with the feel of water on his head. Encourage him to move his arms and legs, protecting him from the surrounds rather than stopping the baby from splashing. A floating toy will give added pleasure and this would be a good time to introduce armbands – to be played with rather than worn. As soon as the baby is ready, transfer him into the adult bath, with an adult in there with him. There the activities can continue and expand. The baby can put

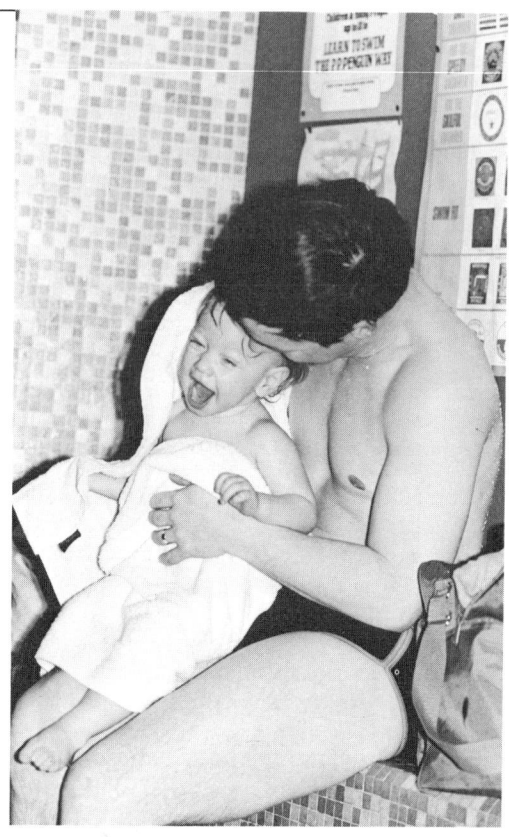

Alleviate baby's fears by appearing happy, keen and smiling

his hands on the bottom of the bath, let his body float and kick his legs. The shallowness of the bath will keep his kicking position horizontal. If the bath is big enough, let him wear his armbands in order to become used to them before progressing to the public pool.

Going to the public pool for the first time can be very frightening to a baby or small child. The echoing noise, the smell, the vast sheet of water, the reflections and the crowds of strangers are too much for

some, so a visit just to watch from the side may be a sensible introduction. *But you must ensure that the baby has had the first set of triple inoculations* because pool water is not a safe environment for small babies without such a protection.

The speed at which a child learns to swim has little to do with his intelligence. The inbuilt sense of self-preservation balanced with the level of inquisitiveness have much more effect. Persevere with the frightened child. Leaving the pool will not remove the problem and may even emphasize the fear of water. The fear is overcome by the baby becoming more familiar with the surroundings. Whatever happens, the parent must appear keen, happy and smiling, and be readily available to the child at all times. Fear in the parent is transmitted through voice, grip or reaction to the child, so if you feel worried, hide it and learn to smile!

Safety is of paramount importance. Do not carry the baby down the steps into the pool because you might slip. Ask someone to help by lifting the baby down to you. See where the pool attendant is standing, so that you may get their help if required. Try to become a competent swimmer yourself and learn how to give artificial resuscitation in case of an emergency. Keep the baby within your depth unless you feel fully competent as a swimmer. The baby is usually out of its depth anyway, unless the pool is very shallow. If the baby swallows a lot of water and becomes drowsy or distressed an hour or so after swimming, take him to the hospital, explain what has happened and they will soon put him right. Make sure that you know the pool rules for taking little ones swimming. The attendant will know. Take your costume, towels – maybe towel dressing-gowns for you and the baby – a changing mat and, if he is still incontinent, plastic pants to prevent the faeces from escaping. Faeces in the pool are unpleasant and full of bacteria. The best buoyancy aids are armbands of the 'two-parallel-air-chambers-all-round-the-arm' variety ('swim trainers'). They stay on even if (as the baby becomes more proficient) air is let out of the outer chamber. Unfortunately,

Do not carry baby down the steps. Ask someone to pass baby to you in the water

armbands tend to restrict arm movement, but they do keep the baby upright and give him freedom to go solo right from the start. Children over one year old may find the 'Polyotter' suits more effective, because they leave the arms free. They are, however, more expensive. Rubber rings on their own, however snug, are not really safe. Babies learn by copying and experimenting, together with plenty of encouragement. The parent's task is to provide the best possible situation for learning, with safe support and encouragement. I suggest that the following are also important: **a respect for water safety;** improved confidence with good sense; balance, propulsion and independence; progression towards free swimming; an opportunity for social and emotional education. I do not expect a child to learn to swim without support until he is about three years old and can stand on the bottom of the pool, but in armbands children can be relatively

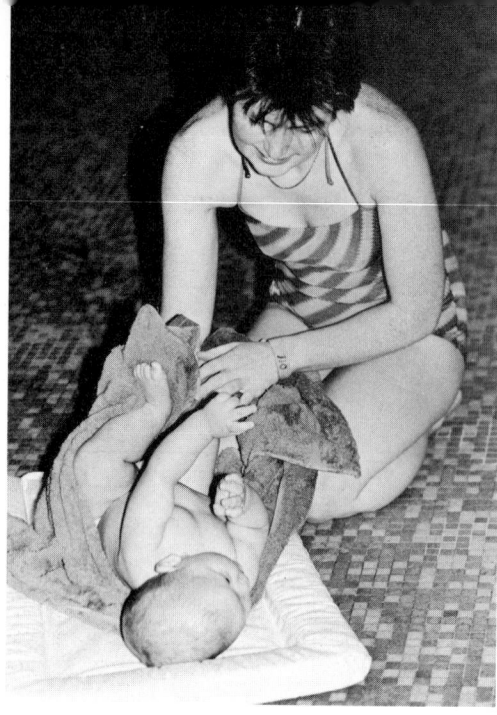

Take a changing mat . . .

. . . and wrap up warm

independent early on, and have a great deal of fun. Once in the pool, let the child go and allow him to float unaided in armbands. Be where he can see your face. If necessary, let him hold onto you; then when he is ready, he will let go – a moment you might have missed if you had held him. If he frets, cuddle him and send him free again. The movements that he will make will be experiments in balancing. Talk to him, keep him company and show by expression, voice and movements what an enjoyable pastime swimming is. If he rolls over, or even goes face-down in the water, move with purpose rather than speed; put him back where he was, give him a smile and a word and send him off again, solo. In time he will be able to balance as he likes, on front or back, and begin to use his legs for propulsion. Let

him sort out his favourite form of kick, either both legs together or alternate. This is the time when Dad and Mum begin to feel redundant, but they are not!

Be patient, watchful and ready at hand to give support. Encourage a good leg kick on front and back by laying the child between your outstretched arms, head towards you, holding his thighs and moving his legs in the correct method. Do this for short periods until he begins to copy it, and demonstrate by swimming yourself. Remember – swim his style! When giving support, and only when necessary, at first hold the baby so that his head and neck are above the water. When the baby shows more confidence, only raise his head, so that his chin rests on the water. Allow the baby to gain strength by holding up his head himself. I end a session by taking off the armbands. The baby finds that the loss of support increases his respect for water. I support him as he lies on his tummy, with my hands either side of his ribcage, fingers underneath and thumbs on top. In this position, he can use his arms and legs to simulate 'swimming'. Once he becomes more confident, see if he will accept 'dunking' (a short down and straight up, completely under water). Slowly count 'One-two-three', blow on the baby's face to make him breath in and then hold his breath, hold him firmly in your arms and go under. Very small babies usually accept this quite happily, while older ones need bubble-blowing and ping-pong-ball-blowing games to practise keeping water out of the mouth. Persevere with only two or three 'dunks' per session. If they are distressed, I approach 'dunking', by jumping in. First I sit them on the side and lift them down, holding them under the shoulders, thence progressively to giving less support, until they jump without help except from their armbands. Ensure that the water is sufficiently deep for them not to hit the bottom.

Progress depends upon the natural skill, physique and temperament of the baby. The following objectives will be helpful:

accept immersion, including water in the ears, mouth and nose; float with armbands, independently, in the vertical, front and back positions; gain and retain balance, and turn at will; exclude water from the nose and mouth; gain confidence and enjoy total immersion; accomplish propulsion using the legs; move independently away from the parent; accomplish propulsion with the

arms and legs; gradually reduce dependence upon artificial support; swim without support on the front, the back and under water; jump from the side; dive from the side (**check depth of water**).

Here are some more activities I have used:

Babies 5–24 months old:

Call the baby's name to encourage turning round; spin like a top; move using 'cycling' with the legs; climb the pool steps; move towards toys; pull the baby through the water on its tummy; ride on the parent's back or tummy; bobbing up and down games; games using Humpty Dumpty, Ring-a-ring-a-roses,

Everybody can swim – it's fun

the Big Ship sails through the Alley-alley-oh, and Pop goes the Weasel; tossing baby into the air (take care here); playing ball.

Children of two years and over:

Splashing games; pat-ball and the like; fetching toys; follow the parent; 'doggy paddle'; towing the child in curves, circles and zig-zags; nursery rhyme games and children's action songs; from jumping, progress to diving; spend more and more time going under water; decrease his dependence on armbands to minimal, especially if he can stand on the bottom; push the child through the water between the parents, encouraging him to swim; swim with a float; increase the distance swum by either trying for a width or counting the strokes achieved.

Babies respond better to encouragement and example than to commands, but parents should insist on progressive practices for some of the pool time if the child is in fact to progress. Play all the time can become aimless. Also, children's standards do not always match our own, which can frustrate a parent who looks for quick results. Don't! **Be patient!** Use your initiative to encourage success, and keep the child happy.

VALERIE LAMBERT

Swimming for People with Disabilities

INTRODUCTION

Many people with disabilities find swimming a very satisfying recreational activity or sport. The reason for this may be because the activities, challenges and teaching methods can easily be adapted to suit a wide range of abilities and personal interests. Three benefits which immediately come to mind are increased safety skills, improved or maintained levels of fitness and an extended circle of friends; but perhaps the greatest, for someone who is non-ambulant, is being able to move independently, to perform feats in water which would be impossible on land. Some people who are handicapped on land become very competent swimmers, far better than many of their able-bodied peers. However, as within any group of people learning physical skills, rates of progress differ. Some with severe learning difficulties may never achieve total independence in water, but this is no reason for them to miss the experience and the fun of water activities within a group. Given that medical approval has been granted, and that there are a sufficient number of helpers and appropriate swimming aids available, I cannot think of any

disability – physical, sensory or mental – which could preclude a person from joining in a swimming session. It really is 'a sport for all'.

My first concern is for people, young and old, with a disability, who are wondering how they may join or choose a swimming class, what they may be expected to do and where it may lead; and for members of a family or friends who want information on behalf of a disabled person.

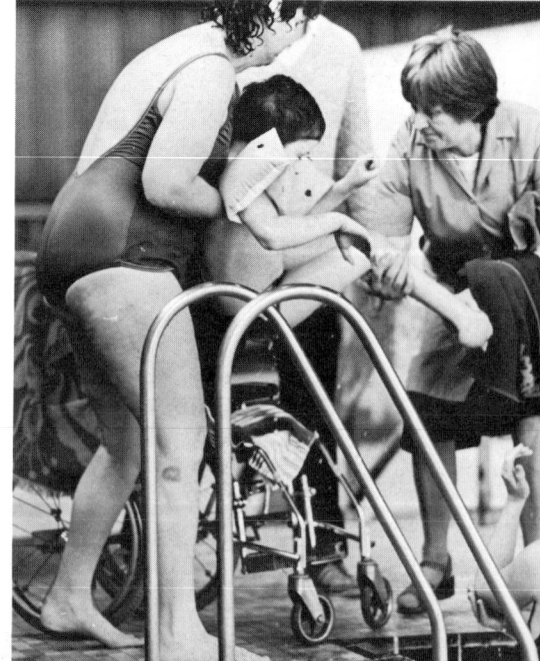

Valerie Lambert has wide experience teaching all age groups. She is an ASA Staff Tutor

MEDICAL CONSIDERATIONS

The first step is to see your medical practitioner to gain written medical approval; *written*, because swimming teachers will request this for their record keeping. Any special considerations arising from your disability should be included, particularly if not outwardly obvious. A teacher needs these details to plan appropriate safety measures and teaching strategies. I cannot stress enough how important it is for you to be frank and honest with your teachers about any aspect of your disability, so that adequate safety precautions can be taken. If you are receiving physiotherapy, then the physiotherapist may have some professional advice to offer too. Swimming sessions may provide another opportunity to practise an activity or action which you find difficult.

While on the subject on gaining medical advice, if you are incontinent it need not be a deterrent to joining a swimming group. Ask the nurse at the local clinic or hospital – or whoever normally advises you – whether the usual procedures need to be adapted if you go swimming; then, when you join a class or club, inform the teacher so that, if necessary, ways of getting in and out of the pool can be selected to avoid pressure on the appliance. Infants and others who are incontinent, who wear nappies or pads and plastic pants, may wear similar clean ones (not disposable nappies) under their swimming costume, but normally just pants and well fitting plastic pants under the costume provide sufficient protection.

CHOOSING A CLASS OR CLUB

The next step is to find a swimming class or club to suit your needs. Make enquiries through friends, the local pool supervisor, the local authority or possibly the library. There may be specialized classes or clubs in your area for people with a specific disability – for example, asthma or severe learning difficulties – or for those with mixed disabilities, or for disabled and able-bodied people together. Specialized classes and clubs will normally be in appropriate venues, usually with specialized equipment, and have teachers with particularly relevant expertise plus a large number of helpers.

If you find you have to look further afield for such a class, there is a comprehensive booklet, *Register of Swimming Clubs and Organized Swimming Sessions for Handicapped People*, 1986, priced 50p, produced by the National Association of Swimming Clubs for the Handicapped, which contains the name and address of the nearest pool and the person to contact, as well as the swimming times of specialized clubs throughout the British Isles and Republic of Ireland.

You may prefer to find an ordinary class, perhaps one for a specific age or ability group. For example, given medical approval, it could be most appropriate for a baby with a disability to join an ordinary parent and baby class, so that the baby can be amongst other youngsters who are likely to constitute the local swimming peer group for a number of years. If the disability promotes the need for some special form of care or communication, then obviously the teacher must be told, but if the other parents are told too, they

will be able to learn what to do and to pass on this knowledge to their children. I have noticed that parents of young children in this type of class are very supportive of each other and each other's offspring throughout the pool sessions.

However, I would recommend that you – or someone acting on your behalf – should visit as many likely groups as pos-

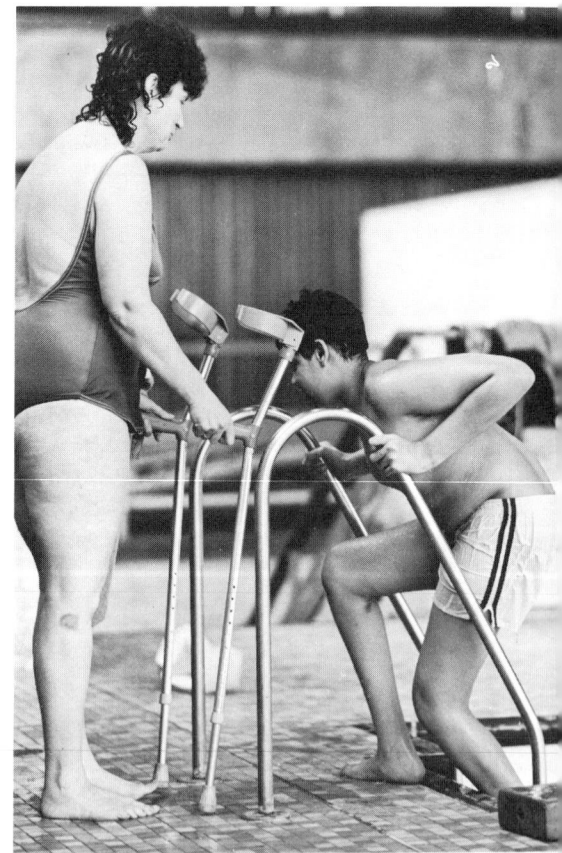

sible so as to draw comparisons. Compare access – if this is likely to be a problem – to, from and within the buildings, including the changing-rooms, and toilets, showers, through to the pool and to the refreshment area; check the space for changing and, if necessary, for a wheelchair at the poolside; also safe storage for a prosthesis, if required. Should you have any doubts, make them known; in one pool I know there is an alternative access route and purposefully designed changing-rooms for handicapped people, not normally mentioned to the general public. Note, also, water and air temperatures; these are usually much higher in special school and hospital pools than in public pools, a factor which will be very important for a swimmer who finds it difficult to keep warm, or to relax unless very warm. Compare the equipment which is available and the ways of getting in and out of the pool. Some pools have ramps, some hoists on which a person may lie or sit, while others have shallow or steep steps. There is also a variety of ways of entering and leaving the water over the side of the pool – from lying, sitting and standing positions, with and without the aid of helpers. When watching, you could be deciding which would best answer your needs.

You could also enquire as to whether the teachers have any special qualifications, for example the ASA Teachers or Advanced Teachers Certificate of Swimming for the Disabled, and whether any of the helpers have the ASA Preliminary Award for Teachers of Swimming for the Disabled, or other relevant awards.

SKILLS TO BE LEARNT

When observing different classes in order to decide which you will join, you may notice that, regardless of the venue or ability of members, all beginners are attempting the same skills, sometimes as isolated tasks, sometimes within fun activities and games. These are safety and watermanship skills which are essential, both for independence in water and as the core foundation for more advanced swimming work: rotation, balance, rhythmic breathing, gaining a safe resting position, propulsion or swimming skills and change of direction.

Water is a great equalizer. All human bodies react in it in the same way: the heavier parts tend to sink lower than the lighter parts. Adjustments can be made to counteract this, simply by altering the body shape or by using swimming aids to increase or decrease the buoyancy of certain parts. Bending the head forwards or backwards will affect the alignment of the trunk, bringing it nearer to the vertical or horizontal – in other words, raising or lowering it. If one side dips more than the other it can be raised by moving one or two limbs in the opposite direction, or turning the head towards the opposite side. Being able to control the alignment of the body and the degree and speed of rotation forwards, backwards and sideways,

may be explored and practised in activities which require twisting or turning, such as when using only one body part to receive and pass on an object to the next person in a team line or circle. (It is advisable to wear socks if the swimmer is unlikely to be aware of the feet scraping the bottom of the pool.)

Rotation and balance are closely allied; the parts of the body which cause rotation may also be used to prevent it. Trying to achieve a balanced static position – stillness – in such a slippery substance as water can be very challenging, but also fun. It is normally easier if the limbs are in the water and body parts are moved

slowly into position, with undue tension. The balance or floating positions most frequently attempted are horizontal or vertical and symmetrical, but they may be at any angle and in any shape. When you have managed to be still in one position, experiment to find others. See if you can keep still for a fixed length of time, or balance while the water is churned up around you by others in the group. Try to create a sequence of balances, rotating smoothly from one to another, perhaps to music, with a partner. Your face may be in the water while rotating and balancing so you will need to practise breath control – not breath holding but relaxed rhythmic

breathing, lifting the head at regular intervals to breathe in and lowering it to blow out into the water through the mouth. Rhythmic breathing is important in all swimming activities, so it is best practised regularly from the beginning. Practise it whenever your mouth is near or in the water. Blowing objects across the surface of the pool and activities or games which include submersion will provide opportunities to practise this skill.

RESTING AND RECOVERY

All swimmers need to be able to achieve a resting or recovery position. For some this may be floating, but for most it means regaining a standing position or, for those who cannot get their feet on to the bottom of the pool, resting on the side rail, the steps, or a raft (if one is in the pool). To change from a horizontal to a vertical position, it is necessary to apply the method of rotation described earlier in this section, moving the head forwards or backwards to tilt the trunk. A faster rotation will be achieved if the legs are curled up towards the chest and then lowered when the body is vertical. Hands and arms can be used to assist the rotation by pressing down or pulling down and forward, towards the sides of the hips, according to whether on the front or back. You may find this easier to do from a prone (on the front) or supine (on the back) position and, therefore, if necessary, can apply your rotation know-

ledge and skill – rolling sideways to be on the back or front, according to which you prefer.

It may be necessary to travel and change direction in order to find a space for taking up a recovery position. You will probably have watched people swimming, showing a horizontal, streamlined body position, with a symmetrical or asymmetrical leg and arm action and rhythmical breathing, all smoothly coordinated. You may learn to do some or all of this in the same way,

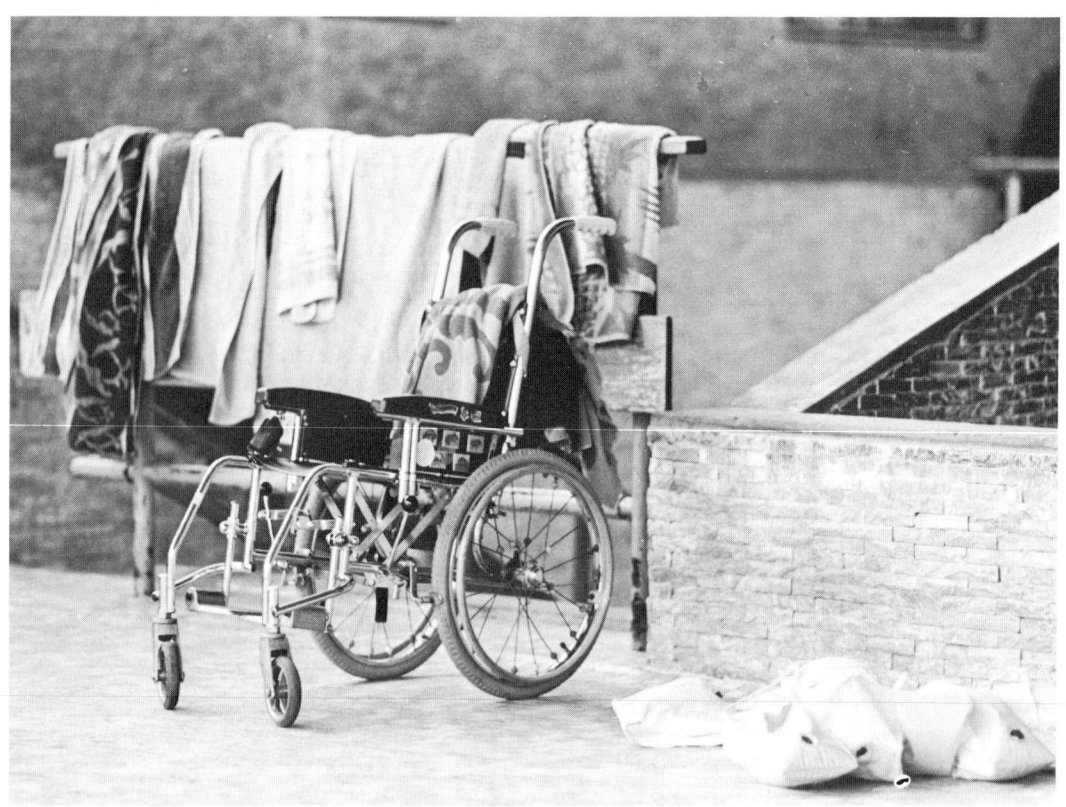

but it is not essential to have two arms or two legs, or to be very flexible or strong, to travel and turn in water. Quite small sculling movements (see page 22) can be used to propel and turn the body in different directions (and to achieve balance). Experiment and find ways of brushing or sweeping the water in the opposite direction to the one in which you want to travel or turn, feet first and head first. You may find you prefer to be on your front or your back. You may also find that you are an underwater swimmer, but this will not be a problem if you have learnt rhythmic breathing. Many able-bodied and disabled children and adults learn to swim under the surface, rising only to breathe in, as another skill. Practise changing direction to negotiate objects and swimmers. Making patterns while swimming, collecting objects and returning them to a set place and taking part in obstacle races are just three ways of developing these skills, but you will find many more in books describing how to teach swimming to beginners.

If you are wondering how you will do all this, remember that it is usual for a disabled person to have a helper who works under the guidance of a swimming teacher. If required, assistance may be given from the moment of arrival at the pool until departure, including supporting and guiding in the water until the beginner can swim confidently and competently. A useful book describing the role of the teacher and helpers, with advice for teaching people with specific disabilities is the ASA publication, *Teaching of Swimming for Those With Special Needs*. It contains a variety of information including many classified activities and games, how to form a club, a book list and numerous useful names and addresses.

THE WAY AHEAD

Having acquired the core skills, your choice of swimming and water activities is wide open. You may want to continue swimming as a leisure and social activity, for maintaining or improving fitness, or to acquire more skills. There are many graded award schemes, for beginners too, through which you can test you progress and gain badges and certificates. You may enjoy competing against others with a similar type of disability, or degree of disability or in open events – perhaps progressing from local to national or even international events. There are other swimming activities to be enjoyed too, such as synchro or water polo, or water sports – skiing, sub-aqua, canoeing, sailing and other boating activities. You may become a helper or the founder member of another club. Look through the other chapters in this book and you will find many activities and challenges for both beginners and competent swimmers which will provide fun and enjoyment – and you, too, will soon experience the sense of well-being that swimming seems to give everyone.

DEREK STUBBS

Nobody is Past It! – Swimming for Fitness in Later Life

Most people now realize the advantages of being just that little bit fitter and slimmer. Whilst there are many ways of bringing

Derek Stubbs is ASA Director of Swimming

this about, swimming must be one of the best exercises for people of all ages, especially as the water supports the body and reduces very considerably the stress on joints which is often evident in other activities.

A BALANCED EXERCISE PROGRAMME WILL:

—improve the overall feeling of fitness and well-being

—improve the functioning of the heart and lungs

—improve strength, stamina and suppleness

—prove enjoyable and become a regular way of life

In this section I aim to give some advice to adults who wish to use swimming as a means of increasing their fitness and sense of well-being; obviously to do this, they need to be swimmers. I most certainly would not want to exclude non-swimmers from gaining the many advantages of regular swimming, and would emphasize that learning to swim is possible at any age and that thousands of adults learn each year. Local authorities, clubs and many other organizations have tackled the problem in recent years, and now there is a successful national 'Adult Learn to Swim' programme. If you are one of the unfortunates who cannot swim, take heart from the fact that most swimming teachers consider it no harder to teach an adult than a child, and that often the self-motivation evident in adult non-swimmers gives them a tremendous start. The earlier sections in Part 1 might be of particular interest to you.

To be beneficial exercise needs to be regular, at least two to three times a week, and moderately vigorous with each session exceeding 20 minutes' duration. Swimming is the best exercise you can undertake to maintain fitness, and it provides an excellent means of getting back into shape when the body had been neglected for a while:

Stamina gives you staying power and endurance, and as it increases you will be able to perform harder and longer before gasping for breath! The fitness of your heart also improves, as it becomes a more efficient machine to send blood full of oxygen and other nutrients to the muscles being used. As you become fitter, your heart will have a more powerful and slower beat.

Suppleness indicates the amount of flexibility in the joints. The greater the range of movement you have, the more efficiently you will perform and the less likely you will be to suffer aches and pains.

Remember that the greater the suppleness, the less chance there is of pulling muscles or straining ligaments.

Strength can be defined as the ability of a muscle or a group of muscles to overcome resistance or create tension – to pull, push or lift. In swimming, it is the power that is needed to propel the body through water, and the speed at which the body travels bears some relationship to strength.

The Health Education Council has published the following table, in which swimming certainly shows up well against other activities; however, it should be remembered that in this context it means fairly strenuous swimming.

S-FACTOR SCORE

	STAMINA	SUPPLENESS	STRENGTH
Badminton	●●	●●●	●●
Canoeing	●●●	●●	●●●
Climbing stairs	●●●	●	●●
Cricket	●	●●	●
Cycling (hard)	●●●●	●●	●●●
Dancing (ballroom)	●	●●●	●
Dancing (disco)	●●●	●●●●	●
Digging (garden)	●●●	●●	●●●●
Football	●●●	●●●	●●●
Golf	●	●●	●
Gymnastics	●●	●●●●	●●●
Hill walking	●●●	●	●●

	STAMINA	SUPPLENESS	STRENGTH
Housework (moderate)	●	●●	●
Jogging	●●●●	●●	●●
Judo	●●	●●●●	●●
Mowing lawn by hand	●●	●	●●●
Rowing	●●●●	●●	●●●●
Sailing	●	●●	●●
Squash	●●●	●●●	●●
Swimming (hard)	●●●●	●●●●	●●●●
Tennis	●●	●●●	●●
Walking (briskly)	●●	●	●
Weightlifting	●	●	●●●●
Yoga	●	●●●●	●

●No real effect   ●●Beneficial effect   ●●●Very good effect   ●●●●Excellent effect

The above chart has been reproduced from *Look After Yourself! Health Guide*, published by the Health Education Council 'Look After Yourself' project.

Improvement in your fitness will not come about with easy swimming – it must be hard, but do not confuse this with speed. Speed is produced as a result of a combination of skill, suppleness, stamina and strength. A skilful swimmer with good technique is obviously going to swim faster with less effort than a non-skilled swimmer who uses much more effort. However, at the end of the day, the increase in fitness is more related to the effort put in than to the time taken to cover a specified distance.

A good guide to effort is to monitor performance, pulse rate and recovery time. Pulse rates and recovery times will be discussed later, but a simple guide to monitoring performance is to learn to use the pace clocks to be found in most swimming pools nowadays. Know your own best times for the various distances and strokes, so that you can note the improvements in your performances; this will give you immense satisfaction.

Bearing the above points in mind you can now develop a methodical approach to your swimming sessions. For example, you might simply swim a set distance or time; or, perhaps, swim a predetermined distance, aiming at a target time. Swimming is ideal for this sort of work; pools are accurately measured to a fraction of an inch, so progression is simple. One important point to remember is to set your own pace. Improvement through greater distance or faster times is a personal achievement and as you progress you will be able to work to your own targets. More people than ever now want to swim regularly, meaningfully and in an organized way.

101

Now we should consider four specific areas:

1 Acquiring or improving swimming skills
2 Starting your training programme
3 The plan – training and timetable
4 Training schedules

1 *Skill*

Without going into great detail, I would simply say that skill means the development of an efficient stroke technique, to which might be added starts and turns. In competitive swimming four strokes are used: front crawl, backstroke, breaststroke and butterfly. There are of course other strokes and, when you are swimming for fitness, any of these can be used to add variety to your schedules. To the four competitive strokes could be added sidestroke, Old English backstroke and inverted breaststroke (sometimes known as life-saving kick), but I would make the point that the four competitive strokes are by far the most efficient.

Stroke technique is covered earlier in the book, but I would like to make the point that improvement of these skills would be much easier with the help of a swimming teacher or coach. Those not attending organized sessions or classes may find difficulty in obtaining the services of teachers and coaches but a knowledge of the strokes and swimming propulsive movements is essential. Thinking and experimenting with technique offers a challenge and can lead to improvement.

2 *Starting your programme*

Most people do not need a medical check-up before beginning a *gentle, gradually increasing* exercise programme unless risk factors are present, e.g. family or personal history of heart trouble, blood pressure, chest troubles, diabetes, dizzy spells or recent illness. However, it is advisable for older people wishing to participate to have a medical check-up and then to *ease into a gradually increasing* programme. Swimming is a relatively inexpensive sport, requiring only a costume and possibly a pair of goggles to get started. I would recommend a nylon or a lycra racing suit – many good brands are manufactured by reputable companies and can be obtained in most sports outfitters. These suits are superior to the more loose-fitting cotton or wool types which are sold in clothing stores. They fit skin-tight, so that you meet less resistance when swimming. They also dry quickly and, if washed after each use, certainly last for two or three years without losing their shape.

Swimmers training for a considerable time with their heads in water would be well advised to wear goggles. These not only prevent sore eyes but give perfect under-water vision, which allows swimmers to see where they are going and makes the whole experience far more pleasant. One point about goggles: adjustment is all-important. For comfort and to prevent leakage, adjust them fairly tightly, using the strap or the nose-piece. Your goggles may occasionally become misted and you can prevent this by using one of several demisting solutions which are on the market. Perhaps the best way is to invest in a pair of anti-fog goggles! These have specially treated lenses which really do resist misting. If you have never used goggles before, you will probably curse them the first time you try them; they may leak, they may become fogged – unless of course they are the anti-fog type – and they may even slip off. Do not be discouraged; using goggles does require a period of adjustment and, after two or three swims, you will see the advantages and never want to swim without them again.

3 The plan

Once you have committed yourself to a planned programme, stick to it. This really builds up to swimming 20–40 minutes three times per week. Unless you are already a regular swimmer start *gently* at first. It does help to keep a record of what you can do in each session, gradually increase the amount of time spent in the water and the distance covered.

The Amateur Swimming Association organizes an excellent Adult Award Scheme which consists of swimming a cumulative distance over a period of time. As an added incentive your training yardage could be logged for one or more of these awards. The need to build up training *gradually* has already been briefly mentioned and how you do this is part of your individual plan. The facts you should consider at this stage are:

—Your own current level of fitness and swimming skills
—The amount of time that you can spare for training per session, and the number of sessions per week you can attend
—Whether you can supplement your swimming training with a few land exercises, i.e. 5–10 minutes per day with flexibility and stretching exercises
—Are you training alone, or with a friend, or in a group?

—Are you intending to have lessons or coaching?

4 Training schedules

This method of planning your training has many advantages over the more casual approach of simply turning up and swimming up and down the pool, sometimes without even a specific distance in mind. If you plan your own training sessions you will automatically start with a disciplined approach and have an incentive to reach your own target. Keep a record of what you have done and remember how you felt when doing it. You then have a base for gradual improvement and increasing the workload. You should also build variety into your schedules; swimming length after length in a meaningless manner can be soul-destroying, so consider some of these points when preparing your schedule to make it more interesting:

—Be realistic in the amount of work you set yourself and the time you can spare
—Start with a gentle warm-up swim, stretching gradually into full stroke extension
—Include three or four different strokes in your schedule
—Introduce stroke drills – these include leg practices, arm practices, breathing practices and stroke improvement drills
—Time some of the swims to give you an idea of how you are progressing (use the sweep hand clocks or pace clocks available in most pools)
—Learn to turn at the ends more efficiently and to push off in a streamlined manner
—Vary the type of session you do. For example, on occasions you could break

your session into five sections as follows:
(a) warm-up
(b) distance work
(c) stroke drills and sectional work
(d) shorter distances swum faster
(e) skills practice, strokes, starts and turns
Occasionally you could swim for a given time and record the distance
—Introduce speed play swims, whereby you increase speed for short periods during a long swim or increase speed into and out of a turn. There are many ways of doing this
—At the end of your training session, allow 2–3 minutes for a quiet, relaxing swim-down before getting out of the water
—The key to success is a regular, consistent and progressive programme. Avoid the temptation to train hard one week and take the next week off. There will be days when you feel tired. Do not despair: if you keep to your programme you will make progress. Generally, work on improving stamina on the days you set longer distances in your schedules and on improving skills and technique on the shorter distance days. Adequate recovery from training is a vital element in successful preparation. Alternate longer sessions and distance work with shorter sessions.

The sweep hand clocks are of tremendous help in timing your swims, rest periods and checking pulse rates, but learn to use them accurately, especially when taking pulse rates. There are two fairly simple ways to check pulse rate. In both instances start the count 10 seconds after

you have finished the swim rather than immediately after, as this slight time lag allows you to prepare and provides consistency. The first method is to count the number of pulse beats for six seconds and then multiply by ten. The second method is to count the number of pulse beats for ten seconds and multiply by six. The first method is the easiest to work out, because you simply add a nought to your count – for example, nine beats in six seconds gives a pulse rate of 90 beats per minute – but the second method is perhaps slightly more accurate. Heart rate target zone training is the best way to approach aerobic exercise. The heart will beat at a maximum speed according to age and fitness. A good approximation is to subtract your age from 220. This will give you your maximum heart rate per minute. To improve aerobic fitness we should exercise at a steady heart rate of 70%–80% of maximum for 20–30 minutes, three times per week.
Exercise heart rate:
—Calculate the maximum heart rate for your age
—During exercise, try to keep the heart rate within the target zone of 70%–80% of that maximum
—Check the working heart rate by counting the carotid pulse (neck) or radial pulse (wrist), using one of the two methods previously described
—Check your recovery pulse one minute after exercising. The larger the difference between work and recovery counts, the greater the indication of fitness
—As your fitness improves, you will have to work harder to keep your heart rate in the target zone

SUGGESTED TRAINING SCHEDULES

To suggest detailed training schedules is not always a good idea because they can be taken out of context when they should be part of a progressive training programme. What may help is a guide to the first four weeks of a training programme showing length of session, number of sessions per week, distances and pace for two different groups. Use these as a guide to suit your own age and fitness levels, but please remember these are *suggestions* for the first few weeks only. You would certainly need to go beyond these, as you should increase your workload progressively for at least a 12-week period.

1   Not-so-fit over 35-year-olds

WEEK 1
Swim once or twice per week.
Swim for 15–20 minutes – fairly easy – cover slightly greater distance on second attempt.

WEEK 2
Swim twice per week.
5 minutes warm-up – continuous swim.
Swim 50 metres fairly hard – rest 1 minute – repeat twice.
Swim continuously for 5 minutes.

WEEK 3
Swim 2/3 times per week.
5 minutes warm-up – continuous swim – use 2 different strokes.
Swim 50 metres fairly hard – rest 45 seconds – repeat 4 times.
Swim continuously for 5 minutes.
Swim 50 metres hard – rest 1 minute – repeat once.
Swim continuously for 5 minutes – use 3 different strokes.

WEEK 4
Swim 3 times per week.
5 minutes warm-up – continuous swim – 3 different strokes.
Swim 100 metres fairly hard – rest 1 minute – repeat twice.
Swim 100 metres – fairly easy pace – second choice stroke.
Swim 50 metres fairly hard – rest for 30 seconds – repeat 3 times.
Swim continuously for 5 minutes.

2 Fairly fit under 35-year-old

WEEK 1
Swim 2/3 times per week.
Swim for 20 minutes – record number of lengths – try to increase distance each time.

WEEK 2
Swim 2/3 times per week.
5 minutes warm-up swim.
Swim 50 metres – rest 45 seconds – repeat 8 times.
Swim 100 metres fairly hard – second choice stroke – rest 1 minute – repeat 4 times.
Swim continuously for 5 minutes.

WEEK 3
Swim 3 times per week.
5 minutes warm-up swim – use 2 different strokes.
Swim 100 metres fairly hard – rest 45 seconds – repeat 4 times.
Swim 150 metres – fairly easy – 50 m of 3 different strokes.
Swim continuously for 5 minutes.

WEEK 4
Swim 3 times per week.
5 minutes warm-up swim – alternate front crawl/back crawl.
Swim 200 metres – rest 1 minute – repeat once.
Swim 50 metres fairly hard – rest 30 seconds – repeat 6 times.
50 metres using legs only – 1st choice stroke.
50 metres using arms only – 1st choice stroke.
Swim 5 minutes continuously.

Most of the swimming, especially the repetition swims, should be fairly hard in an effort to raise the pulse rate to the previously suggested level, but use the warm-up to stretch out and generally prepare for more effort in the main swims. After each session, swim down for a few minutes in a relaxed manner. Occasionally include a 20–30 minute continuous swim and test yourself by comparing the distance covered with previous attempts. This way you can develop your own personal best performances and you have a target for future swims.

COLIN HARDY

Masters' Swimming

INTRODUCTION

From the age of 11 to 23 years, I had trained seriously as a competitive swimmer. However, with job and family commitments and the lack of any incentives my swimming training came to an end. For several years I maintained a minimal fitness level by playing some soccer and tennis, but suddenly my circumstances and outlook changed. I moved jobs and was fortunate enough to have the use of a swimming pool; with the introduction of masters' swimming, I was motivated to re-start my swimming career.

Since Otter Swimming Club organized the first masters' competition at the City University Pool in November 1972, masters' swimming has gone from strength to strength. In 1979 the first Scottish Swimming Tournament took place at Greenock, and in November 1981 the first Sun Life English Masters' Competition was organized by the North-East Counties ASA Management Committee and officials

Colin Hardy MEd, DLC is a Lecturer in the Department of Physical Education and Sports Science at the Loughborough University of Technology; he is also an ASA Coach and Staff Tutor

at York. Sun Life Assurance Society plc have sponsored the English Masters' Competition since 1981, as well as other regional and national events. The masters' swimming calendar now includes many competitions throughout Great Britain organized at club, district and national levels. All masters' competitors are required to be over 24 years of age in the year of the competition, and the age groups go up in five-year bands, i.e. 25–29, 30–34 . . . . 70–74, 75 and over. Pro-

A winning Master is congratulated
Sun Life Assurance Society plc

107

fessionals who are members of affiliated clubs may compete with amateurs 'if the promoter's rules so provide'.

In many masters' competitions, the expert swimmer rubs shoulders with the 'novice' and both young and old share the competitive experience. It is even possible for someone with no particular swimming background to be placed in national masters' competitions. A friend, whose major sport had been table tennis, took up swimming training in his sixties 'to get fit in an injury-free sport'. He has now won medals at different strokes over various distances, including the 100 metres medley where he uses an Old English backstroke. Nevertheless, despite this example, the winners in many of the age groups are frequently the swimmers who had previously competed at county, national and international levels. In fact

The start of a Master's race
Sun Life Assurance Society plc

there is now a group of serious and experienced swimmers who have competed in the USA, Australia and other parts of Europe. More recently some of them took part in the first World Masters' Championships in Tokyo (1986). The first European Masters' Championship is held in Blackpool in 1987.

PLANNING A PROGRAMME AND SAFETY

On many occasions people take an interest in masters' swimming and find appropriate facilities, but cannot get any help in planning their swimming programmes. Therefore, it is important that teachers, coaches and sports leaders – with the help of appropriate texts – are able to give advice on safety, training intensity levels and variety in the programme. All masters' swimmers must be confident in deep water, should have an understanding of and practical experience in life-saving procedures, should know the swimming pool regulations and routines and should have a medical check-up before starting to train. The intensity of the swimming sessions will obviously depend upon the basic fitness of the participant and what he or she is trying to achieve. It is known that an individual's endurance can be improved by swims lasting longer than three minutes at a moderate pace, and by repeat swims at various distances (interval training) where the swim is somewhere between 75% and 90% of maximum speed for a particular distance, and the rest intervals are half as long as the time taken to swim the distance. Target heart rates can be between 60% and 75% of maximum heart rate and this can be increased to 85% after training regularly for six months.

Variety in the programme can be achieved by swimming both competitive and recreational strokes (e.g. side stroke) and practising bi-lateral, catch-up and single arm techniques. Different training methods such as fartlek, over-distance, types of interval work (e.g. negative split, descending sets, broken-swim) and sprints can challenge the masters' swimmer, and the use of pull-buoys, drag belts, rings and suits, pulling tubes, kick-boards, fins, hand paddles and wrist weights add interest to the schedules. To avoid eye soreness and to help with vision, swimmers should persevere with goggles.

At Loughborough time is set aside for a masters' session four times a week throughout the year and individuals attend as frequently as they can. The age range is from 20 to 70 years and includes both men and women. I have devised a progressive training programme with the aim of catering for all the different levels. The idea is that individuals learn about training through information on the schedules and through experience, so that they can eventually construct their own workouts. I give direction and help when required, but I also have time to train at the same session; all members of the group are self-motivated and do not need a coach pacing up and down the bath side. (See tables for example schedules.)

EXAMPLE SCHEDULES

MAIN STROKE: breaststroke

2ND STROKE: elementary backstroke, back crawl

OTHER SKILLS: nil

DISTANCE: 500 metres

EQUIPMENT: float or pull buoy, clock or watch

PHASE	PRACTICE	FOCUS	QUESTION
1 full stroke	swim 100 metres on BREASTSTROKE	Kick and extend the arms beneath the water surface.	Did you manage a short glide?
2 full stroke	swim 100 metres on ELEMENTARY BACKSTROKE	Kick as you pull the hands down from a 'Y' position beyond the head.	Did you get the timing right?
3 part practice	place the float between the upper parts of the legs: pull 2×25 metres on BREAST-STROKE (rest for 20 seconds after the first 25 metres)	Pull outwards and inwards but keep the hands in front of a line dropped from the shoulders.	Could you see your hands out of the 'corners' of your eyes?
4 full stroke	swim 2×50 metres on BREASTSTROKE (rest for 35 seconds after the first 50 metres)	Pull and recover in a continuous action with the hands remaining in front of a line dropped from the shoulders.	Did you feel supported by the arms?
5 full stroke	swim 100 metres on BACK CRAWL	Keep the feet stretched and just break the water surface with the toes at the end of the upward movement.	Did you manage to break the water surface with the toes?
6 full stroke	swim 50 metres on BREASTSTROKE	Extend the arms beneath the water surface and pause for a moment.	Is a short glide part of your technique?

110

MAIN STROKES: butterfly dolphin, back crawl, breaststroke, front crawl.

OTHER SKILLS: nil

DISTANCE: 1000 metres

EQUIPMENT: float or kick board and pull buoy, clock or watch

PHASE	PRACTICE	FOCUS	QUESTION
1 full stroke	swim 200 metres FRONT CRAWL	Recover the arms by lifting the elbows close to the body line.	Are you feeling more mobile in the shoulders?
2 full stroke	swim 200 metres INDIVIDUAL MEDLEY (swim 25 metres each on butterfly dolphin, back crawl, breaststroke, front crawl and then repeat)	Keep the hands moving continuously during the propulsive actions.	Did you lead all arm propulsive movements with the hands?
3 part practice	kick 200 metres INDIVIDUAL MEDLEY (kick 50 metres each on butterfly dolphin, back crawl, breaststroke and front crawl)	Kick vigorously from the hips in the crawl type strokes and forcefully extend and bring the legs together in the breast-stroke.	Did you kick hard?
4 part practice	pull 200 metres INDIVIDUAL MEDLEY (pull 25 metres each on butterfly dolphin, back crawl, breaststroke, front crawl and then repeat)	Increase the speed of the hand movements during the propulsive stages.	Did you pull powerfully?
5 full stroke	swim 4×50 metres INDIVIDUAL MEDLEY: 50 metres each on butterfly dolphin, back crawl, breaststroke and front crawl (rest for 30 seconds between each 50 metres)	Concentrate on maintaining a regular stroke rhythm with a breath every arm cycle.	Are your strokes getting faster?

Everybody can swim – it's fun

MAIN STROKE: front crawl

2ND STROKES: back crawl, elementary backstroke, breaststroke kick in the supine position

OTHER SKILLS: nil

DISTANCE: 1500 metres

EQUIPMENT: clock or watch

PHASE	PRACTICE	PACE	FOCUS	QUESTION
1 warm up, full stroke	swim 200 metres on 2 STROKES: alternate ELEMENTARY BACK-STROKE and BREASTSTROKE KICK in the SUPINE position, changing after each 25 metres	SLOW	Kick with the feet turned outwards and feel the pressure on the insides of the feet and lower legs.	Did you get the feet turned out before the kick?
2 full stroke	swim 400 metres OVER-DISTANCE TRAINING on FRONT CRAWL using a CATCH-UP STROKE	MODERATE	Pause for a moment with both arms in front and extended – you will have to use the legs effectively!	Did you keep the legs moving continuously?
3 full stroke	swim 300 metres FARTLEK on FRONT CRAWL, changing the speed after each 25 metres	SLOW and MODERATE	Change the pace from slow to moderate by speeding up the arm recovery.	Are you finding it easier to change the pace?
4 full stroke	swim 4×50 metres INTERVAL TRAINING on FRONT CRAWL (rest for 25 seconds between each 50 metres)	MODERATE	Keep the pulling action close to the centre line of the body with the palms facing mainly backwards.	Did you keep the palms moving backwards?
5 full stroke	swim 4×25 metres SPRINT TRAINING on FRONT CRAWL (rest for 40 seconds between each 25 metres)	FASTER THAN USUAL	Concentrate on a continuous hand push and arm recovery.	Did you hold a fast pace?
6 full stroke	swim 2×25 metres SPRINT TRAINING on FRONT CRAWL (rest for 1 minute after the first 25 metres)	ALL OUT	Concentrate on a continuous hand push and arm recovery and a continuous hand entry and pull.	Did you go all out or just fast?
7 cool down, full stroke	swim 250 metres on BACK CRAWL	SLOW	Keep the hips close to the water surface and look upwards.	Did you maintain a streamlined body position?

MAIN STROKE: front crawl   **2ND STROKES:** own choice

OTHER SKILLS: nil   **DISTANCE:** 2000 metres

EQUIPMENT: training tube, hand paddles, drag belt, drag suit, float or kick-board and pull buoy, clock or watch

PHASE	PRACTICE	PACE	FOCUS	QUESTION
1 warm up, full stroke	swim 150 metres OWN CHOICE STROKE	SLOW	Loosen up the joints.	Do you feel prepared for the next phase?
2 full stroke	swim 300 metres FARTLEK on FRONT CRAWL: alternate moderate and fast swims, changing the speed after each 50 metres	MODERATE and FAST	Sharpen up the propulsive and recovery movements for the fast 50 metres.	Did you maintain the fast pace?
3 full stroke	swim, using a TRAINING TUBE, 250 metres on FRONT CRAWL	MODERATE	Concentrate on continuous arm actions.	Did you keep a steady arm rhythm going?
4 part practice	pull, using HAND PADDLES, 200 metres on FRONT CRAWL	MODERATE	Keep the elbows higher than the hands during the propulsive movements	Did you keep the elbows up?
5 kick	kick, using a DRAG BELT, 150 metres on FRONT CRAWL	MODERATE	Work hard on the upward movements and keep the leg actions shallow.	Did you keep the legs close to the water surface?
6 full stroke	swim 100 metres on FRONT CRAWL	FAST	Move the hands backwards in a curved path close to the centre line of the body.	Did you maintain a fast controlled pace?
7 full stroke	swim 3×50 metres INTERVAL on 55 seconds	FAST	Pull and push vigorously and recover the arms in a fast, controlled movement.	Did you manage this phase?
8 full stroke	swim 8×25 metres INTERVAL on 25 seconds *or* 30 seconds	FAST	Maintain a fast stroke rhythm.	Did you get some rest at the end of each 25 metres?
9 full stroke	swim, using a DRAG SUIT, 250 metres on FRONT CRAWL	MODERATE	Maintain a regular leg kick with steady continuous arm actions.	What difference did you notice?
10 cool down, full stroke	swim 250 metres on any 2 STROKES: organize in any way as long as you swim 125 metres on each stroke	SLOW	Perform the stroke at a speed that just maintains the near horizontal body position.	Did you swim in an easy and relaxed way?

From Hardy, C. A. *Swimming for Fitness – A Progressive Programme.* Health and Physical Education Project, Loughborough University of Technology (1986).

Igor Polianski (USSR), world champion in 1986 for 100m and 200m backstroke

Mary Meagher (USA), 1984 Olympic gold medallist for 100m and 200m butterfly; 1986 world champion for 200m butterfly.

Such schedules can be used by both competitive and recreational/fitness enthusiasts as I feel that the aim of masters' swimming should not be confined to racing. Swimming as a physical exercise not only improves the cardiovascular system, but also keeps muscles and joints in good working order. In addition it can help with weight problems by increasing energy expenditure without a compensatory increase in appetite and energy intake. Training regularly can give you a sense of personal achievement and satisfaction, and it can help you to relax and to get away from the pressures of everyday life.

If masters' swimming is to progress, more pool time and space must be made available; more public swimming sessions should include 'training' lanes, and swimming clubs and community groups must show a greater awareness of these masters' swimmers in their planning. Cooperation with other aquatic bodies such as the Royal Life Saving Society and the British Sub-Aqua Club would offer other opportunities for fit swimmers to gain more water time. In Great Britain, the Amateur Swimming Association has given its support to a club-initiated movement that encourages people to swim regularly. We must now improve the media coverage and convince a wider audience of the benefits of our sport.

Greg Louganis, USA, 1984 Olympic Games Spring- and High-board gold medallist, who gained a record number of points. He is generally acknowledged as the greatest diver of all time.

Part Three: And now for something different

Diving

INTRODUCTION

Diving has given me many exciting challenges. It is a truly fun sport which can be enjoyed by participants of all ages and abilities. The ability to dive adds a new dimension to your trip to the local swimming pool, as well as being an accomplishment which offers great personal satisfaction for those who take up its challenges.

SAFETY

The observation of a few simple common-sense rules will help anyone who wishes to learn or practise diving:

1 You should be able to swim competently in deep water. (This sounds obvious, but if I had a pound for every joker I had seen leap from the boards or poolside at the deep end, and then need fishing out because they couldn't swim, I would be quite wealthy.)

2 If you suffer with ear trouble, or have a cold, don't go diving without first consulting your doctor.

3 Only dive in a **controlled** environment, i.e. the swimming pool, where the depth markers show a depth greater than your own height fingertip to toe at full stretch, **not** into a river or gravel pit where you think you know the depth.

Mike Edge, MIBRM (Dip), DMS (Rec), Former GB and England diver, has been a national coach since 1981, and has coached teams at World, Olympic, European and Commonwealth levels

4 Don't try to rush your learning processes; only take your next step up the progress ladder when you are fully confident that you have mastered the preparation work leading up to that step. I would strongly advise anyone who wants to learn to contact their local pool: the management can usually direct you towards a club or, increasingly nowadays, offer to enrol you on their own instructional courses. Either way, tuition which will guide you safely through your first steps in diving can be obtained.

FEAR

Diving at any level, beginner to Olympian, is all about conditioned reflexes conquering fear. The first fear that needs to be overcome is one of the most fundamental, and that is the fear of having your head completely submerged in water. Anyone who has done a 'belly-flop' will tell you that attempting to dive without putting your head under water can be a stinging experience! Each step up the progress ladder will require the conquering of a new fear, and this is one of the major attractions of the sport. I call it the 'adrenalin kick'. The feeling of achievement that comes with each successfully completed step up the ladder has to be experienced to be believed. If safety rule **4** is always obeyed, then fear will be kept to a manageable level.

THE PROGRESS LADDER

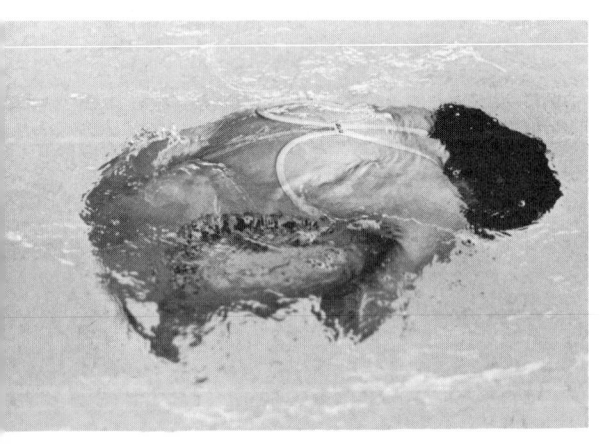

1 Confidence building exercises in shallow water
Learn to get your face wet while keeping your eyes open. There are many exercises that you can work out and try for yourself: for example, standing on your hands in the shallow end of the pool, or picking up objects from the pool floor.

2 Confidence builders in deep water
Get increased pressure on the ears and

Tuck or mushroom float

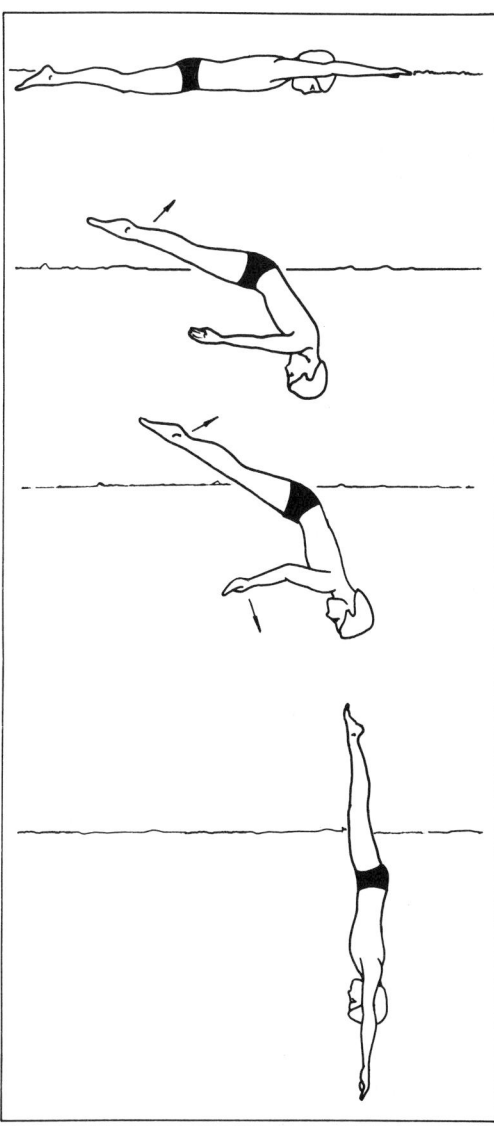

Surface dive

water going up your nose by gliding to the bottom of the pool and pushing up. Just release a little air gently, through the nose, as you submerge, and the pressure will ease. You could also try a surface dive.

3   Basic jumps (deep water)
Place great emphasis on jumping high and maintaining good body tension. Always try to feel what your body is doing. When you jump, if you can feel your legs stretch out on take-off you will probably jump well. When working with Chris Snode (1978 World Cup Diving Champion, Gold Medallist at the 1978 and 1982 Commonwealth Games) on a particularly complex dive, his legs kept slipping apart on the entry. After much work the answer turned

Straight jump

And now for something different

Tuck jump

4 Sitting rolls

These introduce the concept of entering the water head first. Make sure the correct hand position is achieved and maintained so that you learn **safe** habits.

Hold the hands tight, stretch the arms directly above the head so that the head and arms are pointed towards the water, and squeeze the shoulders up to the ears. With your body locked in this position, try to focus your eyes just past your thumbs. This will always give you a clear view of the point of entry. As the name suggests, these exercises start from a sitting position with your heels in the scum channel or resting on the rail, if there is one, the upper body gradually being held more erect as confidence increases.

Correct hand position

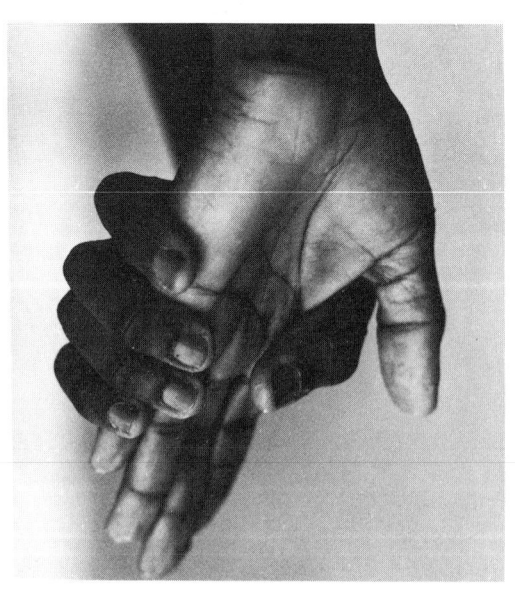

out to be simple: he was not feeling his legs stretch all the way through the water.

These basic jumps introduce the diving positions.

There is also the piked jump, where the body is bent at the waist only. See the picture of Chris Snode on p.125 for pike action in a dive. In all three positions, try to point your toes and ankles. Nothing detracts from good diving practice more than a pair of 'boots'! As these three jumps are mastered, you can turn round and do them backwards (always take care to jump away from your take-off point) and also take them on to the diving boards.

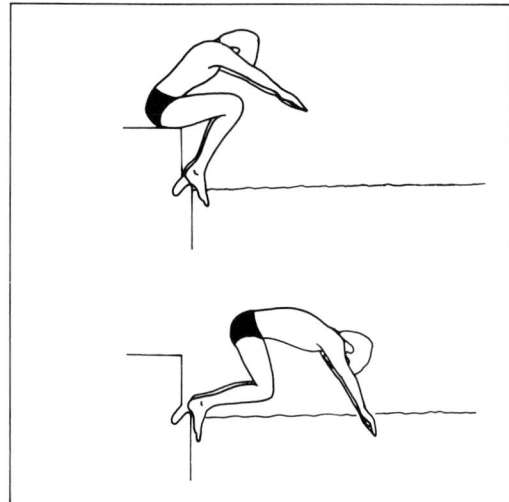

Sitting dive

5   Kneeling roll
Both feet are placed on the poolside, and you roll forward, attempting to leave your feet on the poolside until your legs are straight. Remember to focus your eyes on the entry point. As confidence comes with

Kneeling dive

this step, so the body can be held more erect and the idea of springing can be

introduced so that the rolls becomes dives.

The squat spring is similar to a crouch roll except that the starting position has one foot with toes curled over the edge and the other foot slightly back from it.

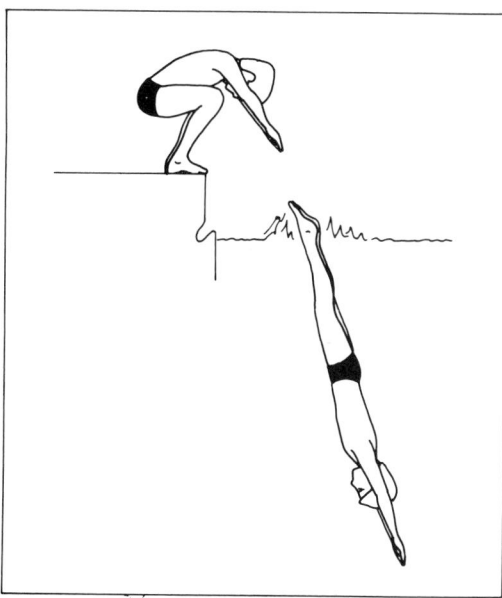

Crouch roll

6   Standing dives
The simplest of these is the pike fall. This is one of the fundamental diving exercises and once mastered can be safely performed from any height of diving board.

The major points to remember with this trick are:
(a) ensure you have the correct hand position
(b) bend from the waist only, trying to keep your back as flat as possible

121

And now for something different

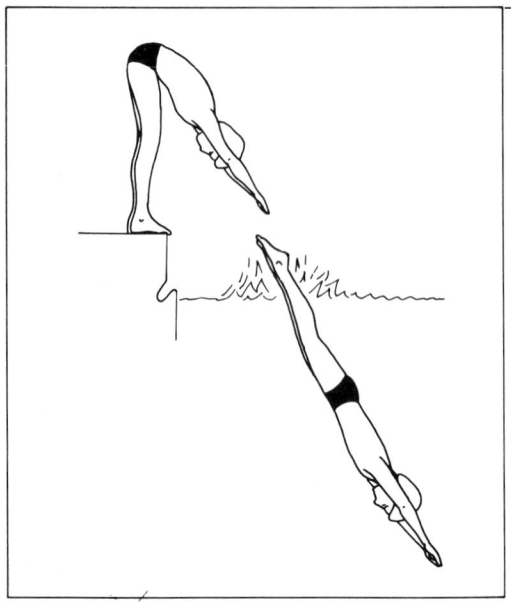

Pike fall

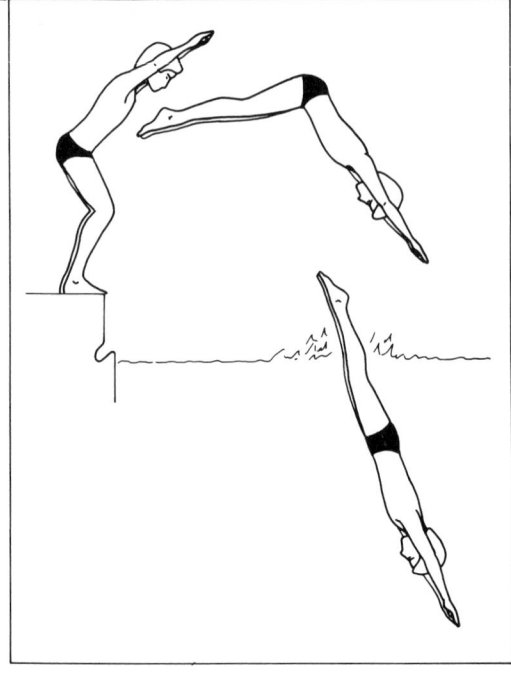

Crouch dive

(c) keep your eyes focused on the entry point
(d) keep your legs straight and just over-balance, do not push
(e) feel your body stretch out full for entry.

7 Springing dives

All of the previous exercises have been worked out to provide progressive experience in body control and actually going in head first. The springing dives are your first real experience of controlling your body, when YOU are providing the major impetus to dive in head first.

Points to remember for a crouch dive:

(a) take up a crouch position, with your body bent forwards at the knees and hips, and your arms extended above your head, showing a straight line from your waist to your fingertips
(b) ensure the correct **safe** hand position is maintained from start to entry
(c) focus your eyes on your intended entry point (about 1 metre in front of the poolside)
(d) when ready straighten the legs, feeling the toes push against the poolside so that your hips are pushed up high
(e) keep your body bent at the hips (piked) and you should have no trouble entering the water head first
(f) as you make your entry, stretch your legs out straight in line with your body, and feel all of your muscles stretch as hard as you can make them.

The spring header is very similar to the previous dive, the major difference being the starting position, which is made with your legs straight and your body bent forwards at about 45 degrees from upright. The springing action is commenced with your legs straight, moving smoothly on to bend your knees and straighten them without pausing, thus producing the required action.

The plain header is also similar to the crouch dive, but is started with the arms in a 'Y' position and the body held upright. Try to keep body movements down to an absolute minimum during the dive and remember to clasp your hands together prior to entry. This second point might not seem so important to you while diving on the poolside, but as you progress to diving from higher boards you will find that the number of headaches you get will decrease in direct proportion to the number of times you **grab your hands together properly on entry!**

Spring header

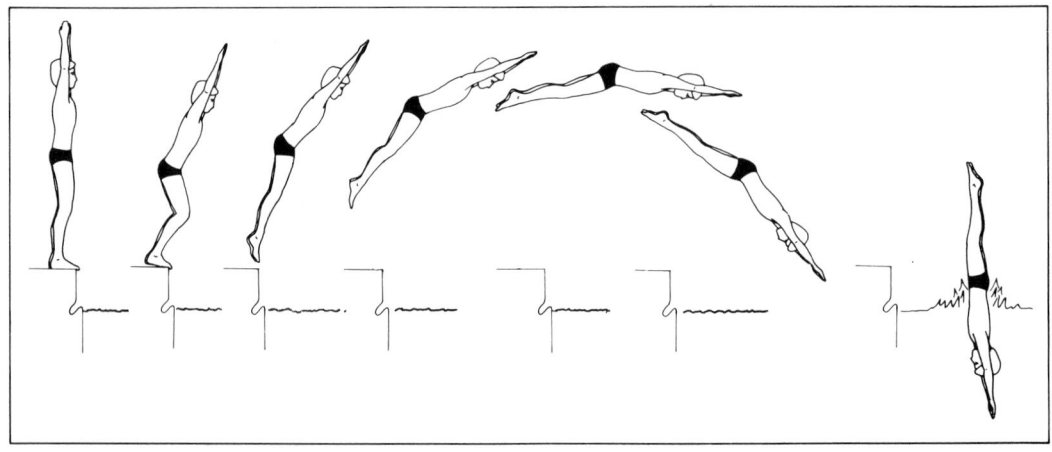

Plain header

PROGRESSION

Whatever your age, physical condition or standard as a diver, it will be worthwhile for you to follow the progression ladder. This will ensure that you have a solid foundation upon which to build any tricks you may wish to learn. If you are still self-taught, having successfully completed all the steps on the ladder, now is the time to investigate the possibilities of joining a club. If you really want to progress to board diving, then I would strongly urge that you **do** join a club: **board diving must be properly supervised**. There are many diving clubs throughout the country and all of them offer a slightly different programme. Try to find one which suits you. Check up on their staff; the ASA have a register of all qualified teachers. If you want to train for competition, then ask about their competitive results and be sure that they indicate the opportunity for adequate progression through club, county, district and national events. Club membership can provide you with a number of benefits over and above going to the pool on your own. The greatest of these is the companionship which comes from a group of people all interested in the same thing. I hope that some of you will get hooked on the sport in the way I did; it has given me the opportunity to travel the world and broaden my whole outlook on life. Good luck and good diving!

(Opposite) Chris Snode, 1978 World Cup diving Champion, Gold Medallist at the 1978 and 1982 Commonwealth Games: here he executes a straight back dive.

Synchronized Swimming

INTRODUCTION

'Synchronized swimming? Oh, I know – you mean water ballet!' If I received a penny every time someone said that to me, I would be able to buy my own swimming pool by now! Originally, the term 'water ballet' was used to describe the slow, graceful formation swimming as seen in many of the old Hollywood movies. Esther Williams – a name most people still associate with this style of swimming – made her fortune choreographing and performing for the camera.

Over the last forty years, synchronized swimming has evolved from water ballet and has become very much more demanding on the swimmer. Although many believe it to be a new sport in this country – probably because of publicity at the Olympic Games – synchronized swimming has been around for rather longer than just two or three years. I am fortunate enough to have been involved for the past twenty years, as both a swimmer and a coach. For me it all started when, as a youngster, I was carted along for lessons at the local pool. I knew 'something was up' when we were driven home in silence. Later that evening I heard my mother

Tracey Ruiz, USA. World Champion 1982

Jane Holland British and European Synchronized Swimming Champion 1973 and 1974; National Coach for the senior squad 1980–84

saying to my father, 'You'll never believe it, but I actually saw someone travelling from one side of the pool to the other with both legs in the air!' I was soon to discover that the pair of legs she had seen that day would change my lifestyle completely.

The interesting thing about this form of swimming is that it can be performed for a variety of reasons and enjoyed at all levels of ability. The fact that it has an entertainment value often attracts wide and appreciative audiences. Clubs can perform Christmas shows and pantomimes, as well as displays for parties and other such functions. Some of my swimmers have become involved in the making of advertisements or videos for pop groups. All of this adds to the scope of a synchronized swimmer and provides many opportunities to use their skills other than in competition. However, as with most sports, if you are serious about competing at a high level you must be prepared to put in many hours of work. Synchronized swimmers are now involved in aspects of training such as weights, flexibility, land-drills (i.e.

Tracey Ruiz and Candy Costee, USA. 1984 Olympic gold medallists for duets

127

walking through routines to check positions and timing on land), and speed swimming, as well as the more specific training of figures and routines. Unfortunately, it is often difficult to find enough pool-time and, for this reason, some clubs provide sessions both in the morning before school and later on in the evening.

However, having managed to put off many prospective participants by this information, I must quickly add that the above times are normally used by the swimmer wishing to do well at a competitive level. Most clubs do hold their classes at more respectable times!

FIGURES AND ROUTINES

I believe that synchronized swimming, as it is today, can be compared most closely with sports such as ice skating or gymnastics. Certain combinations of movements are put together, forming 'figures'. Whereas the skater is required to perform, for example, a 'figure of eight', the synchro swimmer must know how to do a

'back tucked somersault' or a 'dolphin'. For the spectator, the figure section of a competition can be a little boring. However, it plays a very important part in the final results and therefore demands many hours of practice from the swimmer. The

The Santa Clara aquamaids, USA

routine itself is, basically, a sequence which includes a variety of strokes, arm movements and figures, all of which flow from one to the other producing an effect very similar to that of a floorwork composition performed to music by the gymnast. It is possible for a routine to include any number of swimmers from one to perhaps thirty or forty! However, at a competitive level there are three sections: *solo*, *duet* and *team*. A maximum of eight swimmers can swim in the team event, with an extra ½ point awarded for each swimmer over four. The reason for this is simply that the requirements of a routine determine that difficulty increases with larger numbers of swimmers. Consequently, you will rarely see a team of less than eight members at a top competition.

Stipulations in the routine's requirements are laid out, for example the degree of difficulty, synchronization, presentation, interpretation of music and pool pattern, i.e. the area and amount of pool covered. Unfortunately, personal preferences cannot be avoided in sports which rely on human judgement rather than the stop-watch. At times it is apparent that the novelty aspect of a routine can cover up for its lack of difficulty and can, in fact, be very deceptive on a first viewing. At other times, as a coach, I almost feel inclined to ask the judges to get in and demonstrate themselves exactly what it is they want,

when I see a near-perfect figure being awarded only one point more than a 'deficient' one. How frustrating. It is at times like this that I start thinking that perhaps Esther Williams had the right idea after all!

During a competition, one whole point is deducted from the overall total if a swimmer dares to touch the bottom of the pool. Nowadays it is rather unfortunate for some competitors that the TV cameraman always chooses to film below the surface of the water right at that crucial moment when normally a small discreet push might just go unnoticed! Did you know that it is possible for a group of swimmers to lift someone out of the water so that it looks as if she is standing on the surface?

MUSIC

Music has always been a basic ingredient for a routine. It would certainly be wrong to imply that one type of music is more suitable than another; each individual is allowed freedom of choice. Having stated this, there are simple unwritten rules which I find helpful in deciding the type of accompaniment to use. For example, a beginner will cope better with music which has a consistent rhythm. The more advanced swimmer should exhibit versatility of movement and this can be encouraged by the choice of music. I always suggest that my swimmers select music which can be enjoyed by a wide range of people. 'Heavy rock' or 'punk' is unlikely to be appreciated by the judges – not that I am suggesting they are old-fashion, but since they have ultimate control over the number of points awarded it is better to play safe than be sorry! I am certain that some composers would turn in their graves if they could hear how easy it is to 'decompose' their beautiful melodies. With the advancement of music equipment such as cassette players, it is now possible to edit various pieces of music in order to achieve the necessary 'highs' and 'lows' within a 4- or 5-minute routine. However, it is important for this to be done carefully in order to retain the flow of the accompaniment.

How do all the swimmers manage to keep in time, even when they are inverted? I will let you into a little secret – they can hear the music under the water! A small speaker is placed in the water, which is usually sufficiently adequate for sound to be heard almost as clearly as above the surface. When I first began synchro, there were no such things as underwater speakers; instead, one girl on the team would be in charge by blowing raspberries, signifying the timing of the movements to the rest of the swimmers. You can imagine the amusement caused when one of these escaped whilst above the surface!

COSTUMES

Years ago routines were recognized by name, e.g. a team which represented our country at the World Championships were entitled 'Fairground'. The music and movements were chosen in order to portray the title and sometimes stories were told through movement, rather like a classical ballet or an opera; elaborate costumes were designed to fit in with the chosen theme. My first solo was called 'Yellow Bird', after the Hawaiian music – it was so exciting and such a big step forward. I even had the costume made professionally out of gold lurex and it looked very similar to a long-sleeved leotard. To add to the effect there was nylon netting in abundance along both sleeves (as wings), at the back (for a tail), and on my head (the crest). The big moment came I felt just like a world champion. I 'flew' into the water and . . . virtually drowned! The costume became so heavy that it was almost impossible to get back up to the surface – an experience that will never be forgotten!

Since those days themes have disappeared. The swimmer now has free choice over music, and costume design has taken a turn for the better. Fashion suits are found to be much more suitable, since they allow freedom of movement while at the same time looking attractive. During training sessions the swimmers wear a normal training suit with goggles and the frequently mentioned nose-clips without which they would most definitely suffer severe sinusitis. For special occasions costumes are decorated and worn with a head-dress. It is interesting to see that, since the Los Angeles Olympics, many fashion suits seen in the shops are now being decorated in exactly the same way.

COMPETITION

Competitions are held throughout the year for all abilities, from novices through to county, national and international levels. Each rung on the ladder is just as important to novices as it is to those at the top. It is a joy to watch children competing for the very first time – and no mean feat to perform alone, with five people sitting at the edge of the pool staring at your every move as they slide their thumb up (and down!) a scale of 1–10

Not so long ago when synchronized swimming was mentioned in passing conversation, people would frown and declare that they had no idea what you were talking about. Now, though there are still a few misconceptions with regard to what is involved, most people have at least seen it on television or as some function or other. This does save embarassing moments when you start hanging upside down in an attempt to explain what you mean! There are many clubs located all over the country, some of which are attached to a speed swimming section. A quick phone call to the County Swimming Secretary will provide all the necessary information regarding clubs or classes in your area.

I have enjoyed many years in synchro and would not hesitate to recommend it as an excellent way to fitness. It incorporates a disciplined training along with creative and artistic skills and must be one of the most interesting and captivating sports today. Why not have a go?

Alexandra Worisch, Austria, 1981 European Championships

Water Polo

INTRODUCTION

Water polo originated in Great Britain in the 1890s and during the period 1890–1930 it was dominated at international level by a succession of British teams. Although there has been a decline in our international achievements since then, the game is thriving with some 400 clubs and 9,000 players in England. In addition to the hundred or so local leagues, there is a National League with 4 divisions and 40 clubs as well as a thriving Women's Water Polo Competition with 40 teams competing in various leagues. The success of the women's game can be judged from their qualification for the World Championships in Madrid in 1986. Competitions are run at Club, County and District level with teams competing for a variety of ASA trophies at all age levels, and British clubs enter the various European competitions.

Although the game is basically healthy, much needs to be done in terms of the development of a coaching structure which will, in the long term, produce competent, efficient and enthusiastic coaches and players. Water polo is an excellent game which children take to very easily. Unfortunately, however, its development has been hampered in the past by restrictions imposed by local authorities over the use of baths both during public and club time and the attitude of some swimming teachers who believed that playing water polo was detrimental to competitive swimming. However, the situation is changing as the ASA are in the process of developing Coaching Courses in all the Districts and have already updated the examination syllabi to include the latest techniques and tactics from the Continent.

Before discussing the game proper, I would stress that the main ingredient for its successful introduction is enthusiasm, plus the ability to overcome lack of facilities and equipment. Indeed, in many areas the water polo coach has to be a master of improvisation! Water polo can make a valuable contribution to the swimming programme in both clubs and schools long after the euphoria for age group and other competitive swimming dies. As such, water polo players can provide a stable base for the future administration of the club.

Mike Glover, GB Water Polo Coach 1976–1979; GB Youth Coach, European Championships 1983; Secretary, National Water Polo Coaches Association

INTRODUCING THE GAME

When introducing water polo, one should avoid being put off by the complexity of the rules, many of which may be beyond the understanding of both beginners and the 'would-be' coach. Briefly, it is a simple game and its simplicity should be stressed in the early stages. Therefore, the coach should pick out the basic rules and initially ignore the more technical rules and tactics. It is essential that in introducing the game one does not allow the rigid application of the rules to hinder the development and enjoyment of playing for the players. In this respect there is a case for adapting the rules to suit the facilities, conditions and the level of experience of the players to ensure close, exciting games which stimulate the interest and enthusiasm of all concerned.

There is, however, a school of thought which believes that water polo is best introduced through a variety of water ball games which, although they have little resemblance to polo, encourage the interest of beginners. Personally, I do not subscribe to this theory on the grounds that once interest has been generated, one still has to redirect it towards polo proper; also, by a flexible use of the rules it is possible for the coach to cater for all levels of swimming and ball-handling technique within the framework of the game. When introducing the game in clubs and schools we must take into account the age and ability of the prospective players. It is obviously important that they should be able to swim, although I have developed the ball-handling techniques with non-swimmers and found that this gave them considerable incentive to improve their swimming.

THE BASIC SKILLS

Generally speaking, the higher the standard of swimmer the easier they will find the introductory practices. There will be a difference in the approach of schools as opposed to that of clubs. At school level, particularly in those with their own pools, it is possible to introduce the game from the first year to pupils with a wide range of swimming ability. On the other hand, in the swimming clubs – with their heavy concentration on competitive swimming, particularly in the age group competition – water polo will probably be taken up later by a much narrower band with consider-able ability. The basic introductory techniques are very similar.

It is necessary for the coach to organize the pool space according to the ability of the pupils, with the stronger swimmers at the deep end and the weaker ones in the shallow water. The basic techniques to be introduced in the first sessions are:
1 Swimming with the ball
2 Picking up the ball
3 Throwing and catching with one hand only.

In introducing (2) and (3), the coach should emphasis the use of the sloping body position to avoid standing on the bottom. Although all these points are stressed by the coach, one should not expect beginners to adhere rigidly to them at all times.

Using this type of introduction, we have brought in two elementary rules: firstly, that only one hand can be used when throwing and catching the ball and, secondly, that players are not allowed to stand on the bottom. By using these two rules, together with not allowing players to take the ball under the water, it is pos-sible to have an elementary game very quickly. The emphasis is on enjoyment combined with the acquisition of skill. The coach should not forget that the object of playing any sport is basically one of enjoy-ment and that in water polo, as in other team games, technical and sterile coaching devoid of any feel for the game can only result in boredom and a loss of interest. A dynamic and positive approach is essen-tial; be friendly, enthusiastic and enjoy your coaching.

DEVELOPING THE SKILLS

Bearing this in mind the introductory period should develop along the following lines:

1 *Swimming with the ball*
(a) Position of the ball relative to head and arms – stress advantages of correct position
(b) High elbows and fast striking rate – explain need for this aggressive type of swimming
(c) Head up – looking over the ball – to see and be able to read the game
(d) Good leg kick – explain need for this in game situation .

2 *Picking up the ball*
Introduce the various methods, explaining their advantages and disadvantages
(a) Hand underneath ball – scoop it up
(b) Hand on top of ball – pressure – roll hand pick up
(c) Grip and pick up

(d) Push
(e) Flick
During these practices, the coach must emphasize the slope position of the body, with the non-shooting hand sculling and the legs to the side and behind, giving stability and comfort during the exercise.

3 *Throwing the ball*
(a) Body position – slope start. This will vary depending on the type of throw – lob, sling shot or backhand
(b) Pick up ball – preferably with the hand underneath and scoop
(c) Ball just behind line of head. Body slope position. Non-throwing hand sculling
(d) Emphasize use of legs and trunk
(e) Insist on follow through either by slap-ping hand on water or asking the player to be in the swimming position after throw
(f) The shooting arm extends quickly

(g) The ball should be balanced on the base of the fingers and not touch the palm.

4 *Catching the ball*
(a) Soft catch – short soft pass ball caught in front of head
(b) Hard catch – longer harder pass. Ball initially taken in front of head, but cushioned by arm movement and finally held behind head.

In both these methods, the hand goes into the shooting position.

Catching practices include catching from left, right, front, above. When waiting for

(Above left) Italy v. Canada, Olympic Games 1984

(Above) Marking technique

(Left) Body slope position

135

Antonio Aguilar, Spain, 1984 Olympics. The ball under firm control

the pass, stress the need to follow the ball, changing the body position to facilitate the catch.

We have now introduced the four most basic skills of the game. I have gone into these in some detail and I believe that if they are introduced properly and care-

fully, the players will benefit greatly in the future. Lack of skill in the basics is the one big factor which shows in senior players today. Do not be too pedantic about all the above points, you will have many opportunities to emphasize them in succeeding sessions

THE SKILLS IN ACTION IN THE GAME

Having introduced these basic skills, we should afford the opportunity to use them in a game situation. Before the game, certain basic rules must be made clear. In the early stages, rules should not come before enjoyment. The coach must use his discretion in their application.

1 The significance of the referee's flag
Make sure all players know that the colour of the flag shown indicates a free throw to that team, and that unlike football the free throw may be taken immediately it is awarded without a further signal from the referee.
2 Play the ball with one hand only

3 Keep feet off the bottom
4 No taking the ball under
5 No pulling or sinking an opponent, nor holding the ball

With these few rules, it is possible to have a reasonable first game with beginners. The coach should, however, take the opportunity to explain further rules as they may arise, e.g. corners, penalties etc.

As the games go on, it will become apparent that the players lack skill and the coach should use this as a reason to introduce further skill practices in order to improve this aspect of the game.

FURTHER LEARNING

Development of the skills usually proceeds as follows:
—further static passing practices
—static shooting practices
—mobile passing and shooting practices
—the push pass
Ideally, each session should contain a brief revision of previous experience, plus the introduction of some new practices and then a game to give the players an opportunity to use these skills. As the player becomes more experienced, then the content of each session becomes more advanced and the coach should endeavour to build up a repertoire of practices which will enable him to offer a varied session each week. It is essential that in all game-related practices (as opposed to fitness and other practices not used directly in the game) correct technique is emphasized at all times. This is particularly true in shooting and passing practices, where the part played by the trunk and legs in obtaining stability and power should be stressed. In push passes, the elbow should not come back beyond the line of the shoulders, as this will negate the value of this type of pass in enabling the player to use it under pres-

sure. Insistence that players observe the rules of the game in practice is *essential*.

Coaches should always try to relate criticism of technique to the game situation, so that the players realize the value of the practices they are attempting. As the team develops, the coach must ensure that the practices he uses are related to the game situation. This involves the build-up of a static technique to its use under pressure in a simulated game situation. For example, the development of the push pass-shot should be done as follows:

1 Static practice stressing the spread of fingers, inward rotation of wrist until thumb is under ball, slight bending of elbow, good snappy pass with feet up
2 Similar to above, but on the swim
3 Swim in and use the push shot from 4 yards
4 Swimming in pairs and shoot
5 Push pass from 10 yards to sitter. Swim in with partner to receive return push pass and then use push shot
6 As above with marked sitter and being marked on the swim-in.

MORE PRACTICE SESSIONS

This type of development can be used with all passing and shooting techniques, and it does give a more realistic assessment of the players' ability to use a certain skill. Many of these practices can be developed by the individual coach according to the standard of his players.

As the team improves, the practices will become more specialized in order to develop particular aspects of the game. This leads to a period of continuous assessment of the team's needs by the coach, particularly in games, and the development of further practices to satisfy

Austria v. Spain, Olympic Games 1984

4 Marking techniques
(a) on static player, emphasizing the position of defensive player relative to the ball
(b) on moving players, using mirroring techniques on players coming towards them
(c) blocking and sideways movements
(d) directional changes
5 Shooting:
(a) Backhand
(b) Sling shot
(c) Push/flick

these needs. Swimming training – which should be done with and without the ball – begins to play a very important part in the training session. This can be varied by changing distances, strokes and length of repetition. Leg work is very necessary for the development of the big bath game, and specific practices for this should feature in the training sessions. The development of the egg beater or bicycle kick is also an essential technique for future development. The following may act as a guide in this matter:

1 Bicycle kick – using alternative arms
2 Backward jump to intercept
3 Passing practices using right and left hands

All shooting practices to be developed from static, with no pressure to be mobile and be related to the game situation. After static practice of lobs, flicks, tips, push shots, backhands and straightforward shooting, players should be made to develop these shots on the swim and, in the more advanced sessions, under pressure. It is also important to ensure that the position of the shooting player is varied as much as possible, i.e. left, centre, right from 2 yards, 4 yards, 6 yards and half-way. Coaches should take advantage of shooting sessions to develop the goalkeepers' technique, when much work can be done on positioning for various shots. Shooting practices should not be allowed to degenerate into wild 'blasting' sessions which are of no value and border on the dangerous.

THE TEAM

As the team becomes more advanced and starts playing competitive games, the importance of good tactics becomes paramount. The coach will have to develop specific tactical aspects such as 'man up' and 'man down' play. Different types of

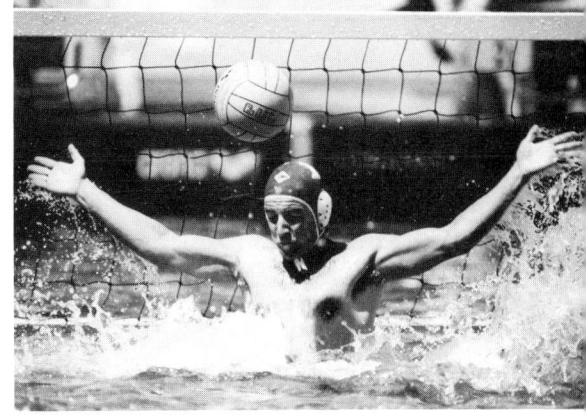

game such as 'press' and 'counter break', use of full and half bath 'presses', rotational play, will all be considered and used by the coach to achieve the full development of his team. However, no team will reach this stage unless good basics have been instilled from the start.

Coaches should encourage their teams to develop a good all-round game relying on tactics and skill, not brute force and ignorance. The value of skill, a pride in performance and knowledge of the rules cannot be over-estimated. Successful teams are those which are encouraged to develop these aspects of the game.

Safety

If you are reading this book from cover to cover, this chapter on Safety may seem to be a 'sting in the tail'. Though swimming is fun, can be enjoyed by all age groups, has a high skill content for those who want to become speed swimmers, and is a multi-disciplinary activity, **at the end of the day someone has to write about the dangers of water and the risk of drowning!** If the safety-conscious reader is expecting a dull list of dos and don'ts, then you are wrong, because this is the opposite of the approach which organizations like the RLSS now advocate.

One of the most remarkable features of research into drowning is that many *good* swimmers lose their lives in the water. This has led the casual observer to wonder if the teaching of swimming leads to overconfidence and to a heightened risk of drowning. Do non-swimmers stay away from the water and avoid this risk? The answer to this question was provided by a research project in the early 1980s which produced figures on the proportion of swimmers to non-swimmers in different age groups in the population of the UK. From this data, it became clear that the drowning rate among non-swimmers may be as much as three times that for swimmers.

Keith Sach, Director of the Royal Life Saving Society UK

So the first piece of good safety news is that **those who can swim have taken a first step to safeguarding themselves in the water**. Everyone, therefore, should learn. However, there *is* a risk to which some swimmers expose themselves quite unintentionally. It arises from a failure to appreciate that the warm, still, supervised water of the swimming pool (where most swimming teaching takes place in temperate areas of the world) is very different to the open water of the seaside, the river, gravel pit or lake. These areas may have a current, may be murky and conceal underwater obstructions, and are almost always unsupervised by lifeguards. Much less obvious is the temperature difference because on a hot summer's day, the prospect of a cool dip is what tempts most people into open water! Can there really be risks associated with this and if so, what are they?

Even in mid-summer, open water rarely rises in temperature above 15°C (60°F); compare this with the likely temperature of an indoor swimming pool, 27°C (80°F), and it's clear that sudden entry into open water is very different to diving into the deep end at the local pool. Research has shown that breathing is massively disturbed by such sudden temperature changes and this factor alone accounts for many, if not most, of the 600-plus drownings each year in Britain. On reflection, this is not so hard to appreciate because

we have all experienced the shock of standing under a cold shower . . . it does, literally, take your breath away, and even a good swimmer is not immune to this shock. So the swimmer who can cover many lengths of the local swimming pool may find that this achievable distance is cut to just a few yards or metres in open water.

There is a wealth of very positive information available on water safety education; much of it is aimed at children and young people, or at those who teach and supervise them. It's based on the belief that prevention is better than cure *and* a conviction that **water safety and lifesaving are best approached as a complementary part of the teaching of swimming.** Information on the sources of such materials is given at the conclusion of this book.

Swimming pools in this country record many millions of bather attendances each year and their safety record is very good indeed. Where lapses occur, they are almost always due to inadequate supervision. More and more domestic (or 'backyard') pools are being constructed in Britain and these place a formidable responsibility for ensuring safety on the owners. It is a great pity that more drownings will take place in such pools before legislation is thought necessary to mirror the regulations in many Australian states which insist on child-proof fencing and gates!

It is recognized that public swimming-pool safety and rescue provision require more than a few warning notices and one or two enthusiastic holders of a long out-of-date bronze medallion. There are training and qualification programmes

now available for lifeguards (the RLSS Pool Bronze Medallion) and for teachers and coaches of all swimming disciplines (the ASA/RLSS Swimming Teacher's Lifesaving Certificate). Over 250,000 people take part in formal water safety, rescue and resuscitation training each year in Britain. The ability to save a life, and the associated skills, should not be regarded as the prerogative of the few. Training is not only a matter of being responsible, it is also great fun. The Sports Council recognizes lifesaving as a sport and a recreation. You are strongly urged to consider improving your skills. Why not use the safety addresses in the following pages to enquire about the way and means of training to help others should you ever be present at a water-based emergency? Remember, to be present and unable to help is both unfortunate and frustrating, **but** to be present and to try to help without training might be very hazardous for **all** concerned. The training you receive could not only help others, it may well teach you to take more care in your own water activities, and so make **you** safer!

The open water of the sea is very different to the deep end of your local pool

ADDRESSES

ENGLAND

The Amateur Swimming Association
Harold Fern House
Derby Square
Loughborough LE11 0AL
Tel: 0509 230431

The Royal Life Saving Society UK
Mountbatten House
Studley
Warwickshire B80 7NN
Tel: 052 785 3943

WALES

The Welsh ASA
National Sports Centre for Wales
Sophia Gardens
Cardiff CF1 9SW
Tel: 0222 397571

SCOTLAND

The Scottish ASA
Airthrey Castle
University of Stirling
Stirling FK9 4LA
Tel 0786 70544

IRELAND & NORTHERN IRELAND

The Irish ASA
Norman Green
6 Maywood Crescent
Dublin 5
Tel: 31 34 76

AUSTRALIA

Australian ASA
Suite 21a
56 Neridah Street
Chatswood
New South Wales 2067

RLSS Australia
PO Box 321
St Leonards
New South Wales 2065

CANADA

Canadian ASA
333 River Road
Vanier City
Ontario

RLSS Canada
64 Charles Street East
Toronto
Ontario M4Y 1T1

INDIA

Swimming Federation of India
3552 Darwaja's Khancha
Shahpur
Ahriedabad
India 380 001

NEW ZEALAND

New Zealand ASA
PO Box 11–115
Wellington
New Zealand

RLSS New Zealand
264 Armagh Street
PO Box 13–489
Christchurch
New Zealand

FURTHER READING

SWIMMING AND FITNESS – GENERAL

ASA, *ASA Handbook*, ASA (Annual publication)
ASA/Savlon, *Babes in the Water*, ASA (1984)
ASA, *The Teaching of Swimming*, ASA (1985)
Counsilman J., *Science of Swimming*, Pelham Books (1968, 9th impression, 1982)
Eady R., *Successful Swimming*, Chas. Letts & Co. (1982)
Harrison J. (ed), *Teaching of Swimming for those with Special Needs*, ASA (1986)
Health Education Council, *Look After Yourself Health Guide*, HEC 'Look After Yourself' project
Maglischo E. W., *Swimming Faster*, Mayfield Publishing Co. (1982)
Sparkes D., *Swimming for All*, Pelham Books (1985)

Verrier J., *Swimming*, Crowood Press (1985)
Whitehead N., *Conditioning for Sport*, A. & C. Black (1985)
Wilson C., *Swimming, Learning, Training, Competing*, Chancerel Publications (1977)

SYNCHRONIZED SWIMMING

ASA, *Synchronized Swimming – A Club Guide*, ASA (1985)
ASA, *Synchronized Swimming Handbook*, ASA (1985)
Elkington H. & Chamberlain J., *Synchronized Swimming*, David & Charles (1986)

WATER POLO

Barr D. & Gordon A., *Water Polo*, Educational Productions (1980)

DIVING

Gray J., *Diving Instruction*, ASA (1978)
Rackham G., *Diving Complete*, Faber & Faber (1975)
Still S. & Carter C. A., *Springboard & Highboard Diving*, Pelham (1979)

LIFE SAVING & WATER SAFETY

Royal Life Saving Society, Handbook, *Life Saving*, RLSS, published in eight separate parts:
1. *Life Saving & Water Safety: An Introduction*
2. *Water Rescue Skills*
3. *Teaching Water Safety (A Project Approach)*
4. *Life Saving Teachers' Guide*
5. *Resuscitation & First Aid*
6. *The Aware Schemes*
7. *Life Guard Manual*
8. *Examiners' Guide to the Award Schemes*

Rick Cross qualified at Loughborough. He has been a LEA adviser and head of teaching studies at a college of higher education. Now a freelance lecturer and consultant in education and recreation, he recently returned to competitive swimming as a Master. He is also a member of various ASA committees and an ASA staff tutor.

Photographs by Allsport Photographic Ltd. Other Allsport contributors include Robert Martin, Tony Duffy, Michael King, Mike Powell, Steve Powell and Dave Cannon. Photographs © Allsport Photographic Ltd 1987

The chart on pages 100–1 has been reproduced from *Look After Yourself! Health Guide*, published by the Health Education Council 'Look After Yourself' project, whose kind permission is gratefully acknowledged.

The photographs on pages 107–108 are reproduced by kind permission of the Sun Life Assurance Society

All line illustrations are reproduced by kind permission from the ASA publication, *The Teaching of Swimming*

Designed by Peter Ward

First published 1987 by Pan Books Ltd,
Cavaye Place, London SW10 9PG
9 8 7 6 5 4 3 2
© The Amateur Swimming Association 1987
ISBN 0 330 29725 2
Photoset by Parker Typesetting Service, Leicester
Printed and bound in Great Britain by
Richard Clay Ltd, Chichester, Sussex